FOREWORD

There is something about tracing the routes of Roman roads that seems to bring out the archaeologist in all of us. Generations of walkers have wondered at the effort and engineering that went into creating these remarkable linear routes through difficult and often hostile terrain.

As this book illustrates, in recent years technological advances in geophysical and remote sensing techniques have added considerably to our understanding of the infrastructure laid down by the Roman armies as they advanced across Wales.

The Roman Roads Project, grant-aided by Cadw and carried out by archaeologists from the four Welsh Archaeological Trusts, undertook a pan-Wales investigation of the Roman roads of Wales. The investigators drew on a range of information sources including the spectacular aerial photography of the Royal Commission on the Ancient and Historic Monuments of Wales. The result has been a comprehensive reassessment of the evidence for Roman roads.

This beautifully illustrated book provides both an introduction and guide to the Roman roads of north-west Wales. I congratulate all those responsible for its production.

Dr Kate Roberts
Head of Archaeology, Cadw

CONTENTS

A high-resolution geophysical survey of the fort at Llanfor shows in great detail the complete plan of the wooden buildings in the early campaign base. Post-holes and individual rooms in the buildings are clearly visible.

10nT

0nT

-10nT

METRES

0   100

PREFACE

When I suggested to Cadw that it might be a good idea to carry out geophysical surveys around one or two of the Roman forts in Gwynedd as part of Gwynedd Archaeological Trust's grant-aided work programme, I had no idea that ten years later my colleagues and I would have re-examined almost all of the Roman archaeology in the county.

Geophysical survey proved to be a startlingly effective technique for examining Roman fort environs. It showed that Roman forts were merely the centre of a wider Roman military landscape and were surrounded by annexes, settlements, official buildings, roads and industrial areas. The most spectacular results came from Llanfor where a large wooden fort produced one of the clearest and most detailed geophysical surveys that I have ever come across. The fort was almost certainly the main campaign base for the invasion of north Wales.

The project was taken up by the other Welsh archaeological trusts and ended up producing large amounts of new information, and was soon seen as the most significant development in Roman archaeological field-work for many decades. The project was expanded, initially in Clwyd and Powys and then in Gwynedd and the rest of Wales, to re-examine the road system.

The Trust's records contained many accounts of Roman roads from a wide range of sources. Not all of these were reliable and several, often contradictory, routes have been proposed for almost all of the Roman roads in the county. Our task was to assess all of the accounts and then see if the roads survived in the field. At the end of the project we had a much clearer idea of the survival of Roman roads in north-west Wales, and could also see where the major gaps in our knowledge were. All of the results were entered into a database that can be accessed via Gwynedd Archaeological Trust's Historic Environment Record. An in-house report was also produced containing detailed maps and a gazetteer.

The results of the forts and roads projects were a catalyst for the production of an entirely re-written edition of the standard textbook on Roman military Wales, *Roman Frontiers in Wales and the Marches*.[1] Unlike the earlier editions, this contained a summary of Roman roads in Wales. There was not, however, space for a detailed examination of each separate road.

We receive a lot of enquiries about Roman roads. I have delivered lectures and guided walks to many societies and organisations and have often been asked where people can read about the results of our Roman road project. The in-house report is rather long and impenetrable, and contains an account of just about everything that has been written about Roman roads in Gwynedd, including a lot of repetition and information that we can now dismiss as being incorrect. My aim in this book is to collect all the information about Roman roads that we are fairly certain is correct and present it in an easily accessible fashion.

DAVID HOPEWELL
Roman Roads Project, Gwynedd Archaeological Trust

---

1 Burnham BC & Davies JL (eds), 2010. *Roman frontiers in Wales and the Marches*

ACKNOWLEDGEMENTS

The Roman Roads Project was funded by Cadw and I would like to thank Mike Yates, Siân Rees, Kate Roberts and Ian Halfpenny for supporting the project. The book draws together information from many sources both published and unpublished.

Of particular importance is the on-going collaborative work between the current researchers into the Roman roads of north Wales. New discoveries are constantly being made and information has been freely passed around, allowing us to evaluate each other's discoveries and debate the merits of various routes. The following researchers have therefore all contributed to the project, to Gwynedd Archaeological Trust's Historic Environment Record and to this book in many ways.

Hugh Toller, based in London, has been one of the main driving forces behind research into Roman roads in Wales over the last few decades and has brought a wealth of knowledge and experience to the discipline. Toby Driver, team leader of the Royal Commission on the Ancient and Historical Monuments of Wales aerial reconnaissance team, has followed up many possible and often tentative discoveries on the ground with superb aerial photographs. Bryn Gethin, based in Warwickshire, has pioneered the use of lidar imagery in this field. Particular thanks are due to John Burman, based in north Wales, who participated in almost all of the project fieldwork, geophysical survey and more recently, evaluation of lidar surveys. He also appears as a distant figure in many of the photographs in the book.

Thanks are also due to Kathy Hopewell, Hugh Toller and Bill Errington for reading and commenting on the manuscript and Philip Steele for further corrections. Macsen Flook transcribed the detailed map backgrounds from aerial photographs. David Alexander kindly posed on a chilly autumn day for the image of the late first-century AD auxiliary infantry soldier shown on the back cover. Thanks are also due to Andrew Davidson, Chief Archaeologist at Gwynedd Archaeological Trust, for help and forbearance during the longer than expected publication process.

Finally, many thanks to Robert Williams who produced a handsome volume from a somewhat daunting collection of maps, photos, drawings, references and text.

David Hopewell

BOUNDARIES, COUNTIES & ARCHAEOLOGICAL TRUSTS

Gwynedd Archaeological Trust was founded in 1974 and is one of four similar Archaeological Trusts which operate across Wales. It is an educational charity as well as being a limited company.

North-west Wales historically consisted of three counties, Anglesey, Caernarfonshire and Merionethshire. These were amalgamated in 1974 into the county of Gwynedd. The boundaries of the counties of Wales were again reorganised in the Local Government (Wales) Act 1994. In 1996 the Isle of Anglesey became an independent unitary authority and the remainder of Gwynedd largely retained its previous boundary, although there were some minor changes. The four Welsh Archaeological Trusts continue to operate within the 1974 boundaries.

The present study is limited to the pre-1974 Gwynedd area and any references in the text refer to this entity. The term north-west Wales is used to refer to a more general geographical area.

A milestone was found overlooking the Menai Strait on road RR67c, SH67897274. (See page 27). The original milestone **>** is part of the British Museum collection and a replica now stands on the site.

The inscription reads
IMP[erator] **CAES**[ar] **TRAIANUS HADRIANUS AUG**[ustus] **P**[ontifex] **M**[aximus] **TR**[ibuniciae] **P**[otestatis] **V P**[ater] **P**[atriae] **CO**[n]**S**[ul] : **III A KANOVIO M**[ilia] **P**[assuum] **VIII**.
   'The Emperor Caesar Trajan Hadrian Augustus, high priest in his fifth year of tribunician power, father of his country, thrice consul : from Kanovium 8 miles.'

A second replica is displayed in the Gwynedd Museum, Bangor.

© THE BRITISH MUSEUM

6

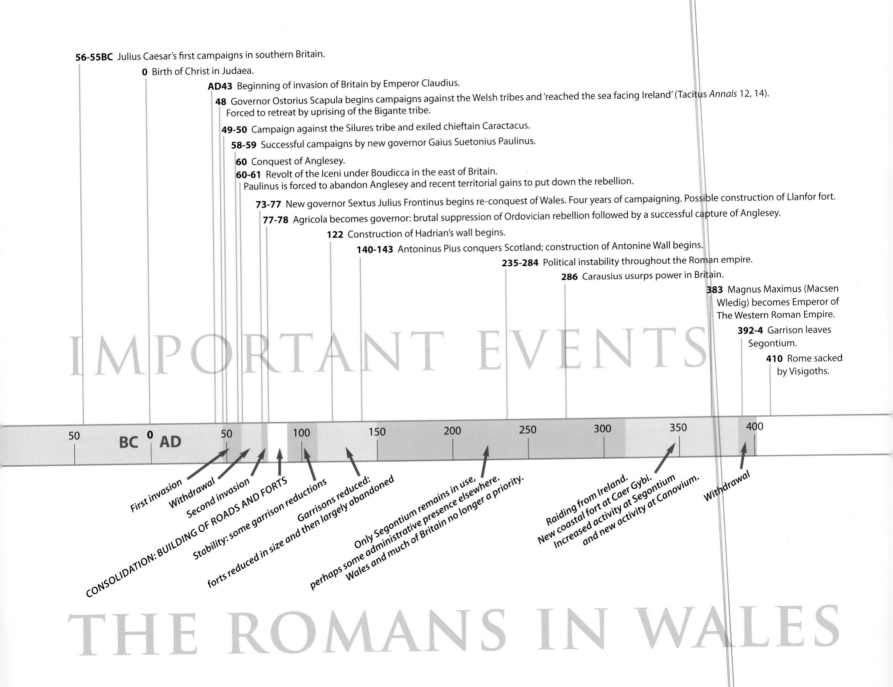

IMPORTANT EVENTS

56-55BC Julius Caesar's first campaigns in southern Britain.

0 Birth of Christ in Judaea.

AD43 Beginning of invasion of Britain by Emperor Claudius.

48 Governor Ostorius Scapula begins campaigns against the Welsh tribes and 'reached the sea facing Ireland' (Tacitus *Annals* 12, 14). Forced to retreat by uprising of the Bigante tribe.

49-50 Campaign against the Silures tribe and exiled chieftain Caractacus.

58-59 Successful campaigns by new governor Gaius Suetonius Paulinus.

60 Conquest of Anglesey.

60-61 Revolt of the Iceni under Boudicca in the east of Britain. Paulinus is forced to abandon Anglesey and recent territorial gains to put down the rebellion.

73-77 New governor Sextus Julius Frontinus begins re-conquest of Wales. Four years of campaigning. Possible construction of Llanfor fort.

77-78 Agricola becomes governor: brutal suppression of Ordovician rebellion followed by a successful capture of Anglesey.

122 Construction of Hadrian's wall begins.

140-143 Antoninus Pius conquers Scotland; construction of Antonine Wall begins.

235-284 Political instability throughout the Roman empire.

286 Carausius usurps power in Britain.

383 Magnus Maximus (Macsen Wledig) becomes Emperor of The Western Roman Empire.

392-4 Garrison leaves Segontium.

410 Rome sacked by Visigoths.

50 BC 0 AD 50 100 150 200 250 300 350 400

First invasion

Withdrawal

Second invasion

CONSOLIDATION: BUILDING OF ROADS AND FORTS

Stability: some garrison reductions

Garrisons reduced: forts reduced in size and then largely abandoned

Only Segontium remains in use, perhaps some administrative presence elsewhere. Wales and much of Britain no longer a priority.

Raiding from Ireland. New coastal fort at Caer Gybi. Increased activity at Segontium and new activity at Canovium.

Withdrawal

THE ROMANS IN WALES

THE ROMANS IN NORTH-WEST WALES

AT THE BEGINNING of the first century AD the tribes of north-west Wales had probably heard rumours of the powerful Roman Empire that was spreading across the continent. The discovery of a first- or second-century BC Mediterranean lead anchor stock off the Llŷn peninsula suggests that there had been contact and probably trade with Europe for many years.[2]

Roman writers recorded the names of at least some of the tribes in Wales. It seems likely that the Ordovices inhabited much of central and north-west Wales, with the Deceangli in the north-east and the Demetae, Silures and Octapitae in the south, with possibly a tribe called the Gangani on the Llŷn peninsula. Of course there was no such country as Wales in the Roman period, but an area similar to the current principality could be seen, even in Roman times, as a geographical and to some extent political region, defined by its uplands and relative inaccessibility.

Julius Caesar's campaigns in the south of Britain in 55 and 54 BC probably made little impression on the tribes of the western seaboard. Things changed considerably in AD 43 with a concerted move to subjugate Britain under the Emperor Claudius. The first incursions were against the tribes of southern Britain, but Wales was an early target and the Roman historian and senator Publius Cornelius Tacitus (AD 56–117) records in his *Annals*, *Histories* and *Life of Agricola* a series of campaigns within Wales starting in AD 47. These were initially against the Deceangli in the north-east and the Silures in the south-east but refugees would have soon arrived in the north-west bringing news of the invasion. The campaigns in the south of Wales continued for around ten years. Caractacus, a chieftain from southern Britain who had been defeated at the beginning of the invasion and was a thorn in the side of the Romans, had taken refuge with the Silures. These proved to be formidable opponents and Roman territorial gains were slow. There seems to have been a breakthrough in AD 58-60 and the campaigns culminated in the well-known attack on Anglesey in AD 60 led by the governor of Britain, Gaius Suetonius Paulinus, and recorded by Tacitus.[3]

> [Paulinus] *prepared to attack the island of Mona which had a powerful population and was a refuge for fugitives. He built flat-bottomed vessels to cope with the shallows, and uncertain depths of the sea. Thus the infantry crossed, while the cavalry followed by fording, or, where the water was deep, swam by the side of their horses. On the shore stood the opposing army with its dense array of armed warriors, while between the ranks dashed women, in black attire like the Furies, with hair dishevelled, waving brands. All around, the Druids, lifting up their hands to heaven, and pouring forth dreadful imprecations, scared our soldiers by the unfamiliar sight, so that, as if their limbs were paralysed, they stood motionless, and exposed to wounds. Then urged by their general's appeals and mutual encouragements not to quail before a troop of frenzied women, they bore the standards onwards, smote down all resistance, and wrapped the foe in the flames of his own brands. A force was next set over the conquered, and their groves, devoted to inhuman superstitions, were destroyed. They deemed it indeed a duty to cover their altars with the blood of captives and to consult their deities through human entrails.*

Paulinus' victory was short-lived. He had barely begun to consolidate the newly-won territory when he received news of the great uprising of the Iceni and their allies under the leadership of Boudicca. He immediately withdrew his forces from Anglesey and marched to Londinium. He finally put down the rebellion in a famous victory somewhere on the line of Watling Street. He did not

2 Boon GC, 1975. 'Roman Caernarfonshire', *Archaeology in Wales* 15 p.44
3 Tacitus, *Annals* 14.30 (translated by Church and Brodribb, 1876)

return to Anglesey and it is presumed that most of the territorial gains were lost. Tacitus' account is just about all the evidence that we have for this campaign in north-west Wales; no archaeological sites have been definitely attributed to this period.

The turbulent happenings of the 50s and 60s were followed by a 15-year hiatus and north-west Wales seems mostly to have been left to its own devices. This all changed with the accession of Emperor Vespasian in AD 69, the first of the dynamic Flavian dynasty in Rome. A new governor, Sextus Julius Frontinus, led a second invasion of Wales and legionary fortresses were built along the border, at Chester, Wroxeter and Caerleon. A large wooden fort at Llanfor may have been a staging post for the attack on the north west. Tacitus records Frontinus' conquest of the Silures in the south and a rebellion of the Ordovices. Frontinus was succeeded by Agricola who brutally put down the Ordovician rebellion and then carried out what appears to have been a surprise attack on Anglesey.[4]

A select body of auxiliaries, disencumbered of their baggage, who were well acquainted with the fords, and accustomed, after the manner of their country, to direct their horses and manage their arms while swimming, were ordered suddenly to plunge into the channel; by which movement, the enemy, who expected the arrival of a fleet, and a formal invasion by sea, were struck with terror and astonishment, conceiving nothing arduous or insuperable to troops who thus advanced to the attack. They were therefore induced to sue for peace, and make a surrender of the island.

This completed the conquest of Wales. The next step was to establish a network of auxiliary forts to maintain Roman dominance over the territory. These were spread across almost all of Wales at a regular spacing of about 20 km. They were linked by the subject of this book: a series of well constructed military roads. It is worth noting that Tacitus is usually quoted when describing exciting battles and conquests. He does however describe Agricola's longer term strategy.[5]

By suppressing these abuses [i.e. aggressive and punitive measures by previous administrators during peace time] *in the first year of his administration, he established a favourable idea of peace, which, through the negligence or oppression of his predecessors, had been no less dreaded than war. At the return of summer he assembled his army. On their march, he commended the regular and orderly, and restrained the stragglers; he marked out the encampments, and explored in person the estuaries and forests. At the same time he perpetually harassed the enemy by sudden incursions; and, after sufficiently alarming them, by an interval of forbearance, he held to their view the allurements of peace. By this management, many states, which till that time had asserted their independence, were now induced to lay aside their animosity, and to deliver hostages. These districts were surrounded with castles and forts, disposed with so much attention and judgment, that no part of Britain, hitherto new to the Roman arms, escaped unmolested.*

In other words resistance and rebellion were first ruthlessly crushed and subsequently the advantages of peaceful coexistence and the opportunities for trade and adoption of Roman customs were promoted. The aim of this strategy, seen throughout much of the empire, was to maintain the conquered territories without constant conflict and heavy garrisoning. Tacitus ends this episode in the life of Agricola with a knowing and cynical statement:[6]

At length [the inhabitants of Britain] *gradually deviated into a taste for those luxuries which stimulate to vice; porticos, and baths, and the elegancies of the table; and this, from their inexperience, they termed civilisation, whilst, in reality, it constituted a part of their slavery.*

There is nothing to suggest that the inhabitants of north-west Wales adopted Roman customs to the extent that Tacitus describes. He was probably describing more Romanised areas such as the south-east of Britain. In contrast, Roman Wales has often been described as a militarised zone with little interaction between the Romans and the local tribes and no uptake of Roman customs. It certainly was immediately after the invasion, but it seems to have become more stable in the second century perhaps as a result of effective peace-time governance. Garrisons were selectively withdrawn from most forts early in the second century, sometimes in response to military commitments elsewhere, but by AD140 almost all the auxiliary forts in Wales had been abandoned or reduced to a token garrison, probably as a result of a push north to the Antonine Wall in Scotland. Segontium was the only survivor in north-west Wales after about AD150.

Evidence is emerging for a degree of integration of the local population in the form of a villa in mid-Wales[7] and an extensive Roman civilian-style settlement on Anglesey at the crossing point of the Menai Strait from Segontium.[8] This was occupied from the late-first century until the mid-fourth century, in other words, for about eight generations.

Garrisons continued to be reduced in the third century, possibly carrying out administrative functions such as tax collection. There seems to have been an increase in strength of the garrison at Segontium in the late-third and early-fourth centuries possibly in response to raiding from across the Irish Sea. A late small coastal fort and watchtowers at Holyhead are probably linked to such threats late in the fourth century. As the Roman Empire began to crumble at the end of the fourth century, troops were withdrawn from Britain. The garrison left Segontium in around AD 392-4, marking the winding down of Roman military occupation in north-west Wales.

4 Tacitus, *Agricola* 18 (*The Germany and the Agricola of Tacitus : The Oxford Translation*)

5 Tacitus, *Agricola* 20

6 Tacitus, *Agricola* 21

7 Davies JL & Driver TG, 2012. 'The First Roman Villa in Ceredigion: A summary report on the discovery and excavation of a late Romano-British villa at Abermagwr, near Aberystwyth, 2010-11', *Ceredigion* Vol.XVI, pp.1-15

8 Hopewell D, 'Excavations at Tai Cochion and Trefarthen', forthcoming, *Archaeologia Cambrensis*

9 Margary ID, 1967. *Roman Roads in Britain* p.22

THE ARCHAEOLOGY OF ROMAN ROADS

The most visible Roman monuments in the landscape of north-west Wales are the series of auxiliary forts built during the consolidation of Roman rule that began in the late 70s AD. The auxiliary forts were usually about a day's march apart (17-20km), and were linked by metalled roads. This road system was designed to be passable in all weathers, and provided vital links between the forts. In the presumably turbulent times after the conquest this would have allowed for the swift passage of reinforcements from fort to fort. In more settled times it would have been important for trade and the use of the *cursus publicus,* the Roman state messenger service. There would have been other roads in Roman times including local civilian roads and tracks and some pre-existing prehistoric trackways, but little is known about these and this study concentrates exclusively on the military road system.

ITER
'route' (*Latin*)

Original Roman sources mention only one road in north-west Wales. The road from Deva (Chester) to Segontium (Caernarfon) appears as *Iter XI* in a register of roads and distances between stations in the Roman Empire called the *Antonine Itinerary.*

Studies of Roman roads in Britain and throughout the wider empire have shown that they were built to a fairly standard design This is of great value when trying to identify the remains of Roman roads in the modern landscape and allows them to be distinguished from most other types of roads and trackways.

The main component of a Roman road is the metalled surface. This is usually in the form of a raised bank known as an *agger.* There are usually ditches to either side of this, acting as drains or soak-aways. In some places in Britain there are cleared, or even metalled, areas to either side of the ditches which are, in turn, sometimes bounded by a second pair of smaller ditches.[9] These secondary features do not, however, seem to be a feature of roads in north-west Wales. A variation on this standard pattern is often seen in the uplands when the road has to run along a sloping hillside. In this case the road is terraced into the slope, sometimes with a ditch on the upper side.

The **agger** consists of a foundation layer and a surface layer with a convex profile. The material for the *agger* in most cases is derived from the local subsoil and one of the characteristics of Roman roads in north-west Wales is a line of quarry pits close to, but not immediately adjacent to, the road. The fact that they are set back a little from the edge of the road perhaps indicates that a strip of land was kept clear to the outside of the roadside ditches in a similar fashion to lowland roads. The foundation layer of the *agger*, where practical, sits directly on the subsoil and may contain some large stones. This method of construction only works where there is a solid substrate close to the surface. In areas of bog, stone slabs or brushwood may be used as a foundation layer to spread the load on top of peat or other soft ground.

The surface layer is most commonly a mixture of pebbles, cobbles and gravel bonded with a variable mixture of silt, clay and sand. It should be noted that there is a common misconception that Roman roads are paved with stone slabs. A survey of Roman roads across Britain revealed that only 4% include any reference to paving and even this may be an over estimation.[10] The most famous paved 'Roman' road in Britain, at Blackstone edge near Manchester, has recently been demonstrated to be post-medieval.[11] A paved road laid on a previous gravel road in the *vicus* at Vindolanda on Hadrian's Wall was itself overlaid by a more conventional running surface of sand and gravel.[12] Paving seems to be an indication of status close to major forts and towns and is certainly not a feature of roads in the wilds of north-west Wales.

Roman roads seem to have been built to fairly standard widths. Hugh Davies plotted the width of metalling of 488 excavated sections of road in Britain on a graph and recognised peaks at the Roman measurements of 15 and 20 *pedes* (Roman feet of 29.6cm) which correspond to 4.4m and 5.9m.[13] Some of the major roads in England are, however, considerably wider than this: Watling Street is on average 10.1m wide. Field observations in Wales indicate that the majority of roads are between 4.5 and 5m wide. In north-west Wales, a few stretches of road appear to be narrower, although none are less than 3m. No roads were found to be consistently wider than 5.5m. Terraces were often found to be closer to 4m wide, but this is probably a result of the inner edge being covered by material that has washed or slumped onto the road.

Another widely held belief is that Roman roads are always straight. When looking at the principal roads running across the relatively easily-traversed terrain of England, this appears to be the case. A similar approach could obviously not be used for any great distance in the uplands of Wales; there are too many cliffs, steep slopes, lakes and bogs. The line of known upland roads shows that the Romans usually took the most direct practical route through the landscape while avoiding most natural obstacles. There are quite often long straight sections but there are also curving

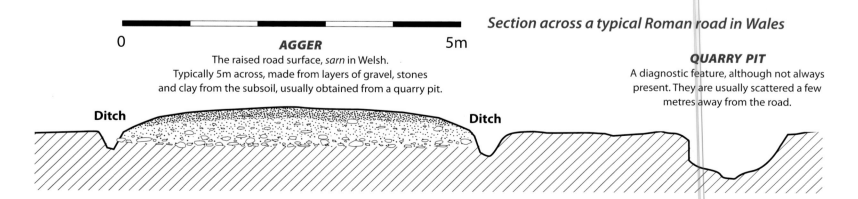

Section across a typical Roman road in Wales

0   **AGGER**   5m

AGGER
The raised road surface, *sarn* in Welsh.
Typically 5m across, made from layers of gravel, stones and clay from the subsoil, usually obtained from a quarry pit.

QUARRY PIT
A diagnostic feature, although not always present. They are usually scattered a few metres away from the road.

Ditch   Ditch

A length of excavated road at Newtown, Powys

sections following the contours around hillsides and there are diversions to avoid obstacles that cannot be easily traversed. The roads avoid steep gradients where possible, but when it is unavoidable, the gradient is lessened by the construction of a zigzag down the slope. When viewed on a large scale map the upland roads usually seem to follow a direct line but at a smaller scale they incorporate small changes in response to the topography. This can be contrasted with many later roads that tend to meander and are often influenced by medieval and later enclosure patterns. Upland Roman roads follow direct routes through difficult terrain indicating that, like the lowland roads, they were well-planned and carefully surveyed in order to find the most efficient way through the landscape. Modern surveyors have, without realising it, duplicated the work of the Romans in a search for the easiest way through the mountains and valleys of north-west Wales; the line of many Roman roads are currently followed by modern gas pipelines and major power lines.

A number of diagnostic features can be used to identify a Roman road:

1 *Its form* : Either a raised agger, or a terrace. The remains of side ditches sometimes survive, or are indicated by lines of rushes or other vegetation.
2 *Its surface* : Gravel and small stones, not paving slabs.
3 *Its width* : Probably 4.5 to 5m. Never less than 3m and rarely over 5.5m in north-west Wales.
4 *Quarry pits* : These are typically set back from the road by a few metres, some may be further away but they are rarely immediately adjacent to the road. They are not always present.
5 *Its route* : Direct, straight if the terrain allows, otherwise as straight as possible. Steep gradients are traversed using zigzags.

A perfectly preserved Roman road will probably have all of these features but a lot could have happened to it in the intervening 1,800 or so years. The most likely scenario is that the road may have continued in use for a long time after the Roman period. If so it would probably not have been maintained and would have become very eroded. Even the best-preserved *aggeres* are usually worn to a point where they are flat-topped; many have been eroded into hollow ways, have been resurfaced or utterly destroyed by later roads. Poorly preserved roads are not easy to verify as being Roman but there are often surviving clues. The later phases of the road may deviate from the original route, leaving fragments of Roman road cutting a corner or even heading off in another direction altogether. Quarry pits may survive, even though the *agger* has been destroyed; in several places lines of pits have been the key diagnostic feature in tracing the line of previously unknown Roman roads.

10 Davies H, 2002. *Roads in Roman Britain* p.60
11 Pearson B, Price J, Tanner V & Walker J, 1985. 'The Rochdale Borough Survey, Appendix 1: Blackstone Edge Road', *Greater Manchester Archaeological Journal* 1 pp.125-31
12 Davies, pp.61-2
13 Davies, p.74

Not all routes continued to be used after the Roman period. Some appear to have been quickly abandoned with little sign of subsequent use as long distance routes. In the uplands, away from intensive agriculture, there is a good chance that there will be significant survival of these roads. This does not necessarily mean that they are easy to find. The *agger* will almost certainly be low and indistinct and may be partly or wholly buried beneath peat. This makes even the best preserved upland roads hard to see on the ground. With good low-angled sunlight they are often easiest to spot from the air, and many recent discoveries have been from aerial reconnaissance.

The task of tracing Roman roads in the lowlands, where land may have been cultivated for many hundreds of years is much more difficult. No roads survive as easily recognisable earthworks in the lowlands of north-west Wales. Fortunately Roman roads can still be detected in these areas. The most common method is using aerial reconnaissance. The remains of the hard-packed gravel *agger* quite often survive within the soil profile without producing a recognisable earthwork. In drought conditions the different drainage and depth of topsoil above the buried road will affect the speed of ripening of crops or cause parching of grass in pasture. As these roads are usually in relatively obstacle-free topography they tend to conform to the classic form of the straight lowland road and can sometimes be seen cutting across the patterns of later fields.

Of course, not every straight parch-mark is a Roman road. All kinds of other, more recent, features such as buried pipelines, old railways and more recent roads can produce similar results and need to be checked for, both on the ground and in archives. The parch or crop mark may give some indication of width, and may even show quarry pits. In many cases, however, a section excavated across the feature may be the only way of conclusively proving its Roman origins.

A few lengths of lowland road survive as barely-perceptible earthworks. These have been discovered either from aerial photographs taken early in the morning or late in the evening, with very low sunlight exaggerating the shadows, or by using lidar (a relatively new surveying technique).

LIDAR is an optical remote sensing technique that uses lasers mounted in an aeroplane to measure the distance to the ground. This builds up a grid of points that can be processed by a computer into a 3D model of the terrain.

Lidar survey is very accurate, allowing very low earthworks to be detected. It has the added advantage of being able to 'see' through some deciduous woodland canopies. It has been shown to be very effective at detecting Roman roads and other archaeological features. Specially commissioned surveys are expensive. Over 68 per cent of England and Wales has, however, already been surveyed by the Environment Agency (EA) and this data has been made available to Cadw grant-aided projects and is available online.[14] This is the focus of ongoing work investigating the route of some of the less well-known Roman road routes. Again careful interpretation is crucial; every straight feature in the landscape is not a Roman road and the same checks and research are needed as for aerial photography.

Place-names can also provide clues to lost sites. The most common Welsh word associated with Roman roads is *sarn*, meaning a causeway that can refer to the raised *agger* of a road, as well as to many other types of features. There are many roads and bridges with a Roman (*Rhufeinig* in Welsh) attribution in their place-names, but this can be misleading. Most areas, according to local traditions, contain at least one 'Roman road'. There is a tendency for any old features, particularly roads, to be labelled as Roman; almost all are post-medieval. It should be remembered that most surviving Roman roads are relatively slight earthworks and do not necessarily conform to the paved straight highway of popular imagination.

Another possible source of information is antiquarian records. Numerous antiquarian studies, tours of Wales and other accounts

---

14 As of April 2013 the Environment Agency in Wales has been incorporated into a new organisation, Natural Resources Wales

PREVIOUS RESEARCH

The study of Roman roads in Wales dates back to at least the seventeenth century with Edward Lhuyd recording several roads reported by his correspondents in the snappily titled *Parochialia: being a summary of answers to 'Parochial queries in order to a geographical dictionary, etc., of Wales'*. Roman roads seem to have held a particular fascination ever since. Richard Fenton records several lengths of roads in his *Tours in Wales* (1804–1813) as do several other writers at the time. Hugh Toller produced a survey of early accounts of Roman roads by Cambrian antiquarians in 2001.[20]

The first attempt to produce a wider account of the Roman roads in Britain was carried out by Thomas Codrington in 1903, but provides little information about roads in Wales.[21] The Ordnance Survey produced their first *Map of Roman Britain* in 1924. An account of the Roman roads of Wales and Cheshire was produced in six volumes by Stanhope O'Dwyer in the 1930s.[22] His map of the county of Merioneth is reproduced below.

O'Dwyer's accounts assembled much of the contemporary information about Roman roads but also collected a lot of spurious accounts and indulged in 'join the dots' style projection of the road routes. His insistence that no metalled roads were constructed between Roman times and the latter part of the eighteenth century inevitably leads to the labelling of any 'old road' as Roman. These accounts include much interesting information about old roads, but the complete lack of any critical fieldwork or application of diagnostic criteria means that they have rightly been regarded with suspicion by subsequent workers in the field.

The first coherent account of Roman roads in Britain that included details of roads in Wales was published in 1955-7 by Ivan Margary in his two volumes of *Roman Roads in Britain*.[23] He devised a numbering system for the roads which is still used today, albeit in a somewhat expanded fashion. This work must therefore be seen as forming the basis for most subsequent studies.

By the 1970s many of the major individual routes in north Wales had been examined in detail with published accounts being produced by Irvine, Jones, Bowen and Gresham and the Royal Commission on the Ancient and Historical Monuments of Wales (RCAHMW) amongst others.[24] In the early 1970s the Ordnance Survey began a programme of work to assess the authenticity of the postulated Roman roads throughout the country. Field investigations were carried out along all of the credible routes and the results were used to update the published Ordnance Survey maps along with the *Historical Map and Guide to Roman Britain*.[25] Only a small proportion of the information from the fieldwork could be added to published maps. The results of the survey are, however, retained in an archive, now held by the National Monument Record in Aberystwyth, as a series of annotated linear maps along with additional notes assessing each route in detail. This archive represents the first thorough review of the Roman roads of Wales.

Further detailed work has been carried out on some roads. Aerial reconnaissance has been shown to be an invaluable tool; Peter Crew and Chris Musson published several aerial photographs with a low angle of incident light that show lengths of upland road in impressive detail.[26] Aerial reconnaissance work continues to be carried out by the RCAHMW. Over the last few decades independent research by Hugh Toller, and various associates has shown that a detailed investigation incorporating aerial reconnaissance, intensive field walking, detailed topographical survey and excavation can be very effective at locating previously untraced roads. Their work on the Caersws to Caer Gai road is particularly noteworthy.[27] Recently Bryn Gethin has been pioneering the use of Environment Agency lidar data for the discovery of previously unknown sites in Wales and beyond.

The most recent major publication is an account of the discoveries of Edmund Waddelove, comprising a detailed account of 'some 200 miles of previously undiscovered Roman roads', mainly in Gwynedd.[28] The evidence for most of these roads was reassessed during the Roman Roads Project. It was found that few of the roads met the diagnostic criteria used by modern researchers. Most were shown to be pack-horse trails, pilgrim's roads or post-medieval trackways. Part of the route between Segontium and Pen Llystyn was, however, confirmed by lidar data. This extensive body of work should not be dismissed but should perhaps be seen as a starting point for further investigations.

26 Crew P & Musson C, 1996. *Snowdonia from the Air, Patterns in the Landscape* 30-1

27 Jones GDB, Putnam WG & Toller HS, 1998. Roman Road, Caersws to Caer Gai *Archaeology in Wales* 38 pp.117-9

28 Waddelove E, 1999. *The Roman Roads of North Wales, Recent Discoveries*

29 Silvester B & Owen W, 2003. 'Roman Roads in Mid and North-East Wales' CPAT Report 527 (unpublished)
/ Hopewell D, 2007. 'Roman Roads in North-West Wales' (Revision 4) GAT Report 668 (unpublished)

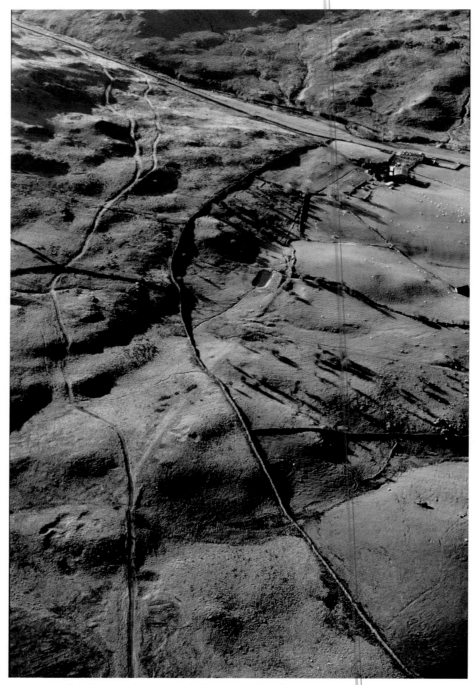

A superb aerial photograph showing the Roman road and extensive quarry pits diverging from the more obvious turnpike road and running through the fields above Cae'r Tyddyn — see page 64   (RCAHMW 95-CS-0833)

THE ROMAN ROADS PROJECT

FIELDWORK AND VERIFICATION

A pan-Wales project examining the Roman roads of Wales was initiated in 2001 and forms part of Cadw's grant-aided programme that aims to ensure that all monuments of national importance receive adequate statutory protection. The initial methodology was established by Clwyd Powys Archaeological Trust and projects based on this were subsequently carried out by the four regional Welsh Archaeological Trusts. Gwynedd Archaeological Trust's project was carried out between 2002 and 2007.[29]

As already described, over the years, a large amount of evidence, of variable reliability, has accumulated relating to Roman roads in Gwynedd. The first task of the project was to collect together all of the information and transcribe the principal routes onto digital maps linked to a database. The linear files produced by the Ordnance Survey in the 1970s proved to be one of the most useful sources of reasonably up to date, detailed information. The information was then assessed for reliability. During the transcription process it quickly became clear that no physical evidence had been discovered for some routes between the forts whereas others seemed to be quite convincing.

The second phase of the project aimed to assess the evidence in the field, using stringent criteria for the identification of Roman roads. These criteria (discussed overleaf) are based on well-established information from sites throughout the Roman Empire with some additional refinement as fieldwork progressed in the uplands. A Roman road can only be verified if there are sufficient characteristics to identify it as such. Ideally this would be a surviving length of *agger* or terrace that is 4 to 5.5m wide, with a gravel surface and side ditches, following a direct line and with associated quarry pits. In practice only a selection of these characteristics are usually visible. Important routes often contain a series of overlying and intercutting roads; a critical examination of the various phases may allow a sequence to be unravelled. For example, a road that exists as a series of eroded hollow ways may have originated as a Roman road. Subsequent use may have all but destroyed the original road but isolated lengths of *agger* and quarry pits may have survived that would be sufficient to prove its origins.

Evidence from crop marks and lidar is more tenuous and has to be carefully examined so that all other possibilities, such as pipelines and more recent features, can be excluded. Clearly a long straight crop mark leading to the gate of a Roman fort could be seen as proven. A similar isolated length would be less certain and would perhaps have to be excavated in order to prove that it is Roman.

Characteristics that are markedly different from those of a Roman road can prove that a road or at least a phase of a road is definitely *not* Roman. Any road or phase of a road that is less than 3m wide, is a hollow way, is paved (unless very close to a fort or town), that meanders without any topographic reason or displays obvious characteristics of a turnpike is not a Roman military road.

It soon became obvious that while some roads were almost certainly Roman, there were others where the evidence was inconclusive. Many offered no physical evidence at all. The varying states of preservation and levels of information were recorded by dividing each road into series of conjoining lengths and allocating each a separate identifying code number in the form of a **PRN (primary record number)**. A new number was then allocated when the characteristics of the road changed. For example, a new number would be given if a road changed from surviving as an *agger* to being adopted by a farm track.

> **Based on the level of confidence that it was a Roman road, each length considered during this project was described and allocated to one of four categories.**
>
> 1 *Known* : A proven road. Usually an extant earthwork or a well-recorded buried feature.
>
> 2 *Proposed* : Conjectural sections either linking known segments or hypothetical road alignments for which there is some physical evidence.
>
> 3 *Predicted* : Virtually no physical evidence for a road other than someone's belief, or a conjectural road alignment with no known traces. Where the authenticity of a road is in significant doubt this is the highest level of status that can be achieved.
>
> 4 *Discounted* : Where a road has subsequently been disproved by a reliable authority or where an alternative line has now been accepted.

The fieldwork produced a good estimate of how much of the Roman road network survives and of how much we know about it. If we assume that all of the known forts were joined by roads and that there was a road on Anglesey, the total length of Roman road must have been about 280km. Only 35km (12.5%) of definite surviving Roman road ('*known*' category) was identified.

A further 104km (37%) showed some physical evidence ('*proposed*'). We can therefore be reasonably confident about the line of about half of the roads in Gwynedd. The rest are practically unknown and exist only as hypothetical lines joining pairs of forts.

There are two areas that are particularly lacking in hard data. The first is the road running south from Brithdir to Cefn Caer, Pennal, in the south of the county. Old roads run to the east and west of a major topographical obstacle in the form of the 893m-high Cader Idris. Neither has been proven to be Roman although some evidence is emerging to support the eastern route. The second is the island of Anglesey which features so prominently in Tacitus' accounts. It seems likely that fortifications were set up on the island during both Paulinus' invasion and the Flavian campaigns. The crossing point from Segontium and the beginning of a road was recently identified near Brynsiencyn (*page 81*), but no military archaeology has so far been identified apart from a fourth-century naval base at Holyhead and two associated coastal watchtowers.

Excavations at the Roman settlement near Brynsiencyn

GAZETTEER : ROMAN ROADS IN GWYNEDD

What follows is an account of the proven or generally accepted Roman roads in Gwynedd.

The roads are named by a number based on the codes that were assigned by Margary in *Roman Roads in Britain*, followed by the names of the forts at either end. The complete lines of the roads are shown on a series of four small-scale maps on pages 23 to 26. Details of surviving lengths of road are then shown on larger-scale maps. These lengths of road are usually in the 'known' confidence category with some of the more intriguing 'proposed' category roads included where appropriate.

The routes of most roads are described in detail along with an account of previous research and the results of fieldwork carried out during the Roman Roads Project. Unproven ('projected' category) lengths are not included on the detailed maps, but the grid-references of significant points are included in the text. Comprehensive references are included as footnotes, in order to maintain the readability of the text. The primary record numbers (PRNs) of most lengths of road shown on the detailed maps are included in the text.

It should be noted that parts of all of the roads pass through private land and permission should be sought from the landowner before visiting them. The portions of roads that pass through the uplands are, in many cases, on open access land and can be walked along without restriction. Current Ordnance Survey Explorer Maps show the extent of open access land and public rights of way. Good examples of Roman roads that can be freely accessed are noted in this gazetteer.

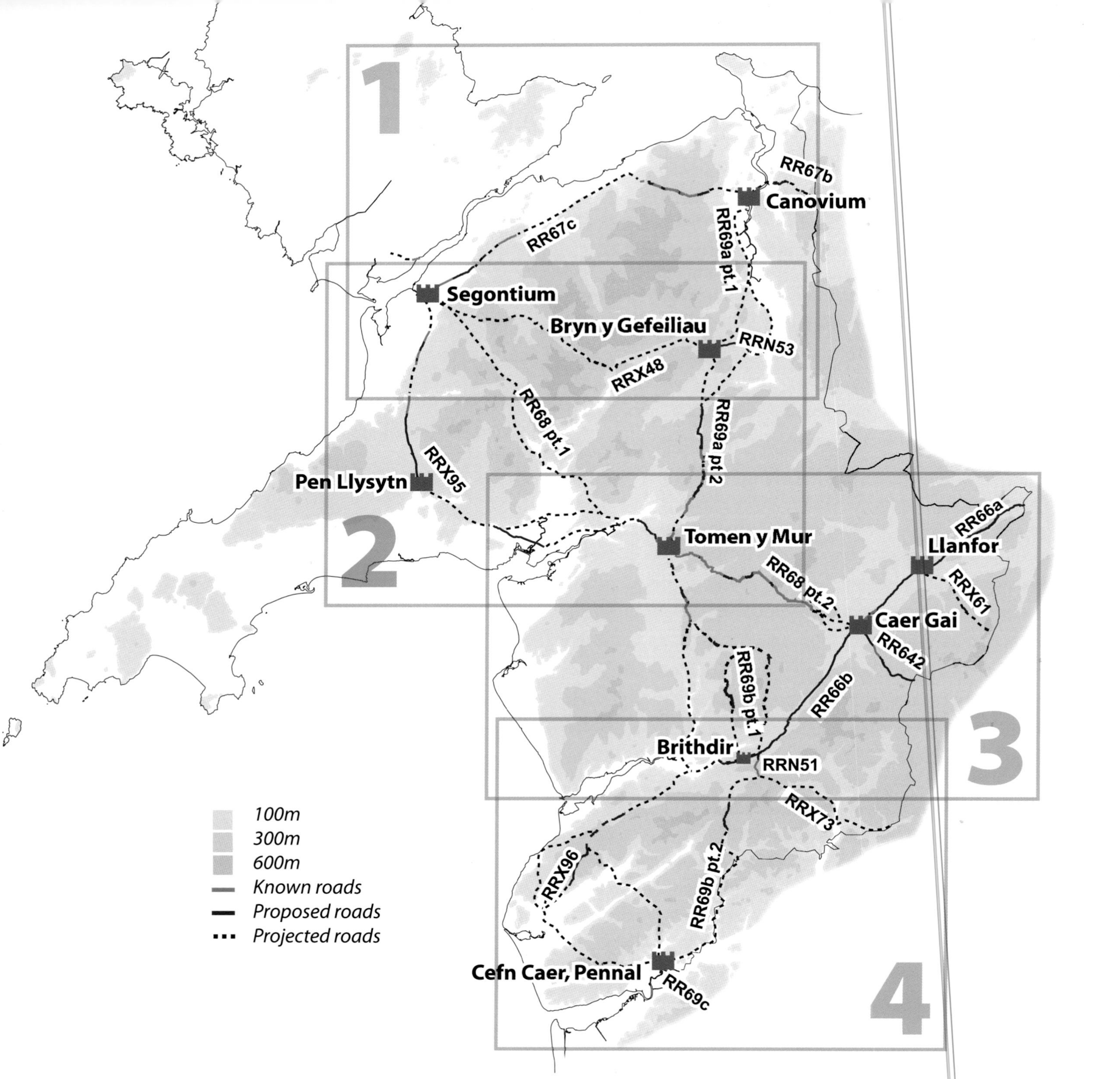

RR67b

Canovium

RR67c

RR69a pt.1

Segontium

Bryn y Gefeiliau

RRN53

RRX48

RR68 pt.1

RR69a pt.2

RRX95

Pen Llysytn

1

2

Tomen y Mur

RR68 pt.2

RR66a

Llanfor

RRX61

Caer Gai

RR642

RR69b pt.1

RR66b

Brithdir

RRN51

RRX73

3

100m
300m
600m
Known roads
Proposed roads
Projected roads

RRX96

RR69b pt.2

Cefn Caer, Pennal

RR69c

4

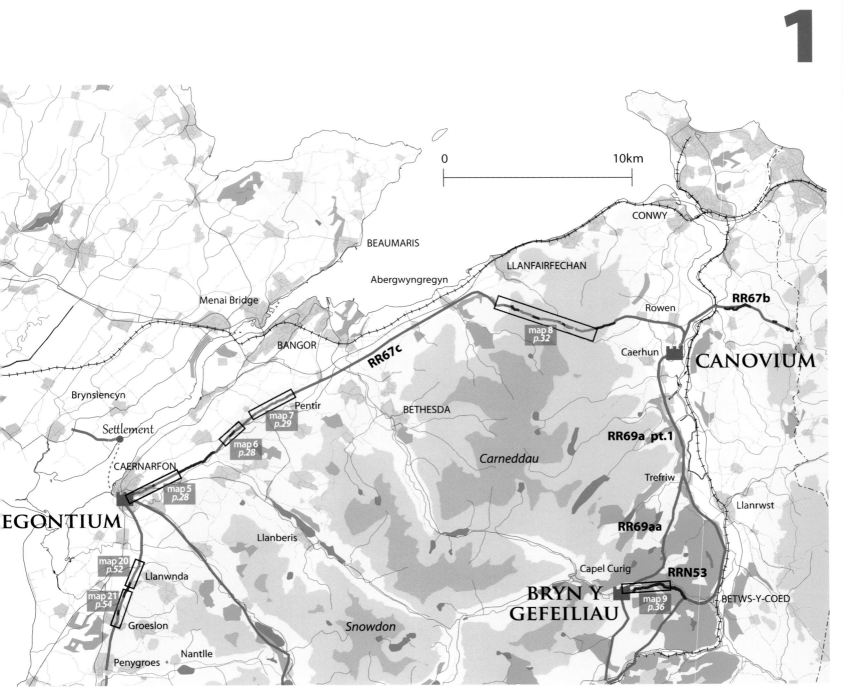

1

SEGONTIUM

BEAUMARIS

Menai Bridge

Brynsiencyn

Settlement

CAERNARFON

Llanberis

Llanwnda

Groeslon

Penygroes

Nantlle

Snowdon

Abergwyngregyn

BANGOR

Pentir

BETHESDA

map 7
p.29

map 6
p.28

map 5
p.28

map 20
p.52

map 21
p.54

RR67c

LLANFAIRFECHAN

CONWY

Rowen

Caerhun

RR67b

CANOVIUM

Carneddau

RR69a pt.1

Trefriw

Llanrwst

RR69aa

Capel Curig

RRN53

map 9
p.36

**BRYN Y
GEFEILIAU**

BETWS-Y-COED

map 8
p.32

0   10km

Contains Ordnance Survey data © Crown copyright and database rights 2012

2

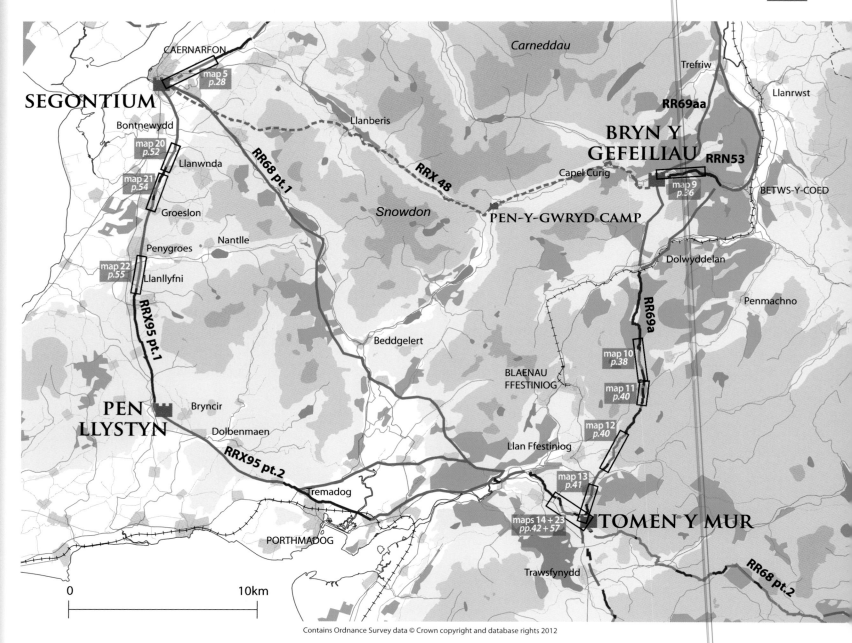

Contains Ordnance Survey data © Crown copyright and database rights 2012

3

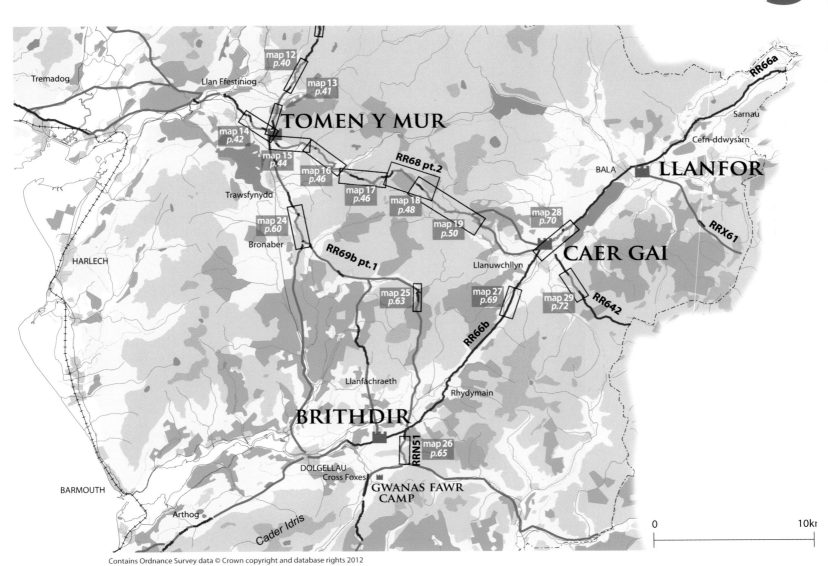

Tremadog

Llan Ffestiniog

map 12
p.40

map 13
p.41

RR66a

Sarnau

Cefn-ddwysarn

map 14
p.42

TOMEN Y MUR

map 15
p.44

BALA

LLANFOR

map 16
p.46

RR68 pt.2

Trawsfynydd

map 17
p.46

map 18
p.48

map 28
p.70

CAER GAI

RRX61

map 24
p.60

map 19
p.50

Bronaber

RR69b pt. 1

Llanuwchllyn

HARLECH

map 25
p.63

map 27
p.69

map 29
p.72

RR642

RR66b

Llanfachraeth

Rhydymain

BRITHDIR

map 26
p.65

RRN51

BARMOUTH

DOLGELLAU
Cross Foxes

**GWANAS FAWR
CAMP**

Arthog

Cader Idris

0   10km

4

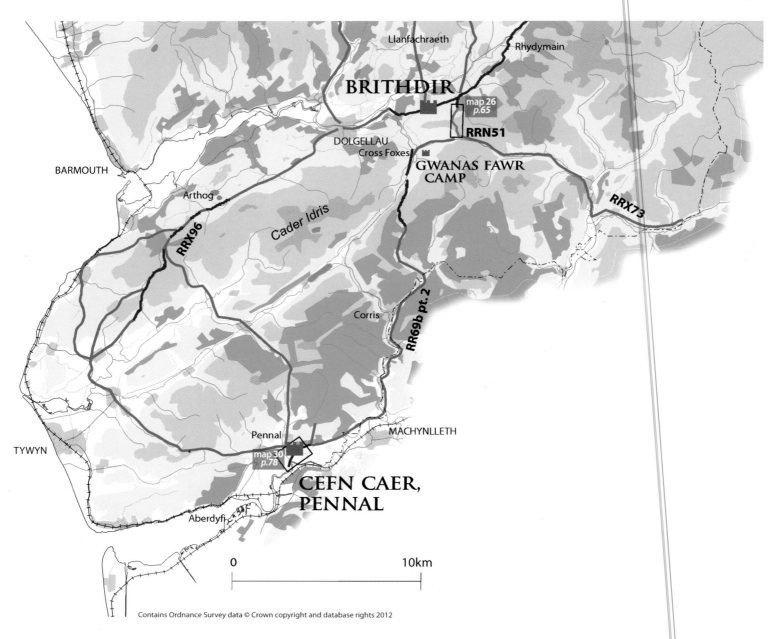

Llanfachraeth

Rhydymain

BRITHDIR

map 26
p.65

RRN51

DOLGELLAU

Cross Foxes

**GWANAS FAWR
CAMP**

BARMOUTH

Arthog

RRX96

Cader Idris

RRX73

Corris

RR69b pt. 2

Pennal

MACHYNLLETH

map 30
p.78

**CEFN CAER,
PENNAL**

TYWYN

Aberdyfi

0   10km

Contains Ordnance Survey data © Crown copyright and database rights 2012

Road RR67c
Canovium — Segontium

Map 1
page 23

The road from Segontium (Caernarfon) to Deva (Chester) is described in the *Antonine Itinerary*. This document was probably compiled during the third century and describes fifteen Roman roads in its British section. The only road described in Wales is *Iter XI* running from *Segontium to Deva* with intermediate stations at *Conovium* in the Conwy Valley and *Varis* (possibly St Asaph). Six milestones have been recorded alongside the road within Gwynedd; one found near Gorddinog (*see page 5*) names the fort in the Conwy Valley as *Kanovium*. Another, found nearby, is illustrated below.

The upper part of a milestone found near Gorddinog is displayed in the Gwynedd Museum, Bangor.

The inscription reads
IMP.P [imperators] **CAES**[ar]
L[ucius] **SEP**[timius]
SEVERUS P[ater] **P**[atriae]
ET M[arcus] **AUR**[elius]
ANTONINUS AUGG
[augustii] **ET P**[ublius]
S[septimius].

'The Emperors, Caesar Lucius Septimius Serverus, Father of his Country, Augustus, and Marcus Aurelius Antoninus, Augustus and Publius Septimius.'

The first part of the route, running east from Segontium, has frustrated researchers for many years. Conjectural routes based on topographical arguments along with occasional alignments of modern features were published by Hemp and Margary,[30] but no definite Roman features were identified. The Roman Roads Project has produced the first hard evidence for the line of the road.

Aerial photograph of the Roman road near Pentir, PRN 17834. The road runs diagonally from the bottom right of the photograph. (RCAHMW AP-2006-3447)

The first evidence was from a series of aerial photographs from two sorties flown in 1986 by J A Story for the Snowdonia National Park Authority. The photographs were taken when the sun was low in the sky and show an intermittent series of very low, linear, earthworks running for 10km to the north-east of Segontium. Additional evidence was then produced by Toby Driver during aerial reconnaissance for RCAHMW in the dry summer of 2006, with well-defined parch marks confirming much of the route (*above*). Further corroboration was provided by Environment Agency lidar data and field walking.

30 Hemp WJ, 1923. 'Environs of the Fort and the Roads' in Hall J P, *Caer Llugwy: excavation of the Roman fort between Capel Curig and Betws-y-Coed* pp.171-5 / Margary ID, 1967. *Roman Roads in Britain* pp.350-1

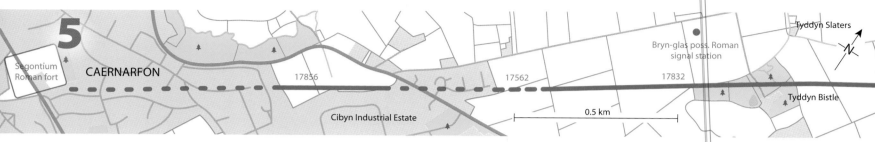

The line of the western part of road RR67c can now be traced with a high degree of certainty, as follows ...

Segontium is surrounded by houses and roads so the line of the road can only be projected through the built-up area for 670m to the east-north-east of the fort. The first evidence for surviving road is a very low *agger* that can be seen on Environment Agency lidar data running through the southern edge of fields to the north-west of Cibyn industrial estate. **Map 5, PRN 17856**. The line then passes through another housing estate to the north-east and then runs in a straight line, passing between Tyddyn Bistle and Bryn-glas, a possible Roman signal station, for 1.5km to Lôn Glai farm. This is can be traced on both aerial photographs and the lidar survey.[31] The landowner confirmed that the feature was not modern. A field visit confirmed the presence of a low *agger* running across several fields. **PRN 17831-2**. The earthwork is difficult to see on the ground in normal conditions; the aerial photograph was taken with a low angle of incident light which accentuated every hump and bump in the field. It is most obvious around **SH50906362** where it is about 5m wide. It has been disturbed in several places, perhaps by drainage works, but appears to be a good example of a Roman *agger*. Ditch cleaning along the field boundaries

to the east of Tyddyn Bistle had exposed the edge of the gravel and clay *agger* in section. Also of significance is a kink in the hedge line and a blocked gateway on the line of the road, suggesting that it once provided a good way across the fields, being slightly raised and therefore drier. The kink probably results from the incorporation of an earlier feature such as a lane or earlier hedgerow into the current boundary.

At Lôn Glai the line has been adopted by a hedgerow and continues in a very straight alignment for a further 0.4km. The name of the farm means Clay Lane in English and may refer to the *agger* of the Roman road. We can be fairly sure about the line of the road up to this point. A lane then continues from Erw-pwll-y-glo for 1.7km to Erw-fforch **SH53016482**. This runs along the contour above a stream and is probably the line of the Roman road, although this cannot be conclusively proven. After a short break this line continues along a direct footpath **SH53686552** shown on the County Series 25" Ordnance Survey maps to the south of Coed-bolyn Lodge. The road, running up to the former rectory at Llandeiniolen, is next recorded by Margary. **Map 6, PRN 17833**. Local tradition and the current residents note that the road can be seen 'when the light is right'. The possible line of the *agger* can be seen both on the Snowdonia National Park Authority's

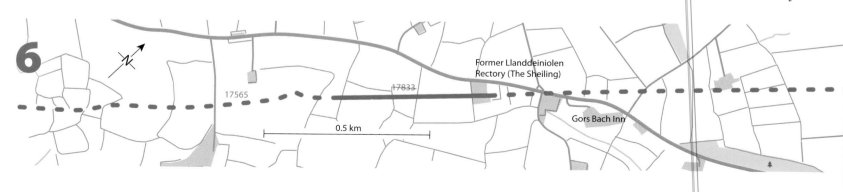

Lôn Glai Farm

aerial photographs and the lidar survey.[32] Four sections were dug across the road in 1966 by pupils of John Bright School, Llandudno. 'No trace of road was seen when the topsoil (12" thick) was removed; clay was found to a depth of 3 feet.'[33] This casts some doubt on the alignment, but there is a possibility that a denuded *agger* (as opposed to a paved road) may not have been recognised as a Roman road.

It is worth noting that a milestone discovered in 1795 has caused some confusion about the line of the road. It was found a quarter of a mile to the north-east of the medieval site called Llys Dinorwig **SH56246318**; this has been confused by several writers with the hillfort of Dinas Dinorwig which is just to the south of Llandeiniolen. The original account in the *Gentleman's Magazine* of 1795 makes it quite clear however:

> *The first is an inscription (not noticed by either Mr Camden or Mr Pennant), supposed to be Roman, lately discovered in the parish of Llanddiniolen, in the county of Caernarvon. The stone was found, and is still situated, about a quarter of a mile to the North-east of an old building called the Llys (described by Mr Pennant[34]), in the remains of several square and circular booths, huts, or cottages, probably the summer encampment of a cohort, or small company of Roman soldiers. Dinorwick, a fortified eminence, universally supposed to be the work of those adventurous people is not above a mile off; and old Segontium no more than six.*

Clearly the milestone was in a hut group, and this seems to be about 3km south of the road. It had presumably been moved from its original position. It is not possible to tell if it originated on the line of the road to the north or if there is an unrecognised side road. A milestone is most likely to have been set up on the main Segontium to Deva road.[35]

There is no trace of the road beyond the rectory for 1.5km. Aerial photographs from the Snowdonia National Park Authority again gave the first hints of a road to the east of Llandeiniolen.[36] **Map 7**, PRN **17834**. A convincing direct route was visible as a low earthwork, but comparison with the 1832 Vaynol estate map showed that some features visible on the photographs coincided with former field boundaries. This cast some doubt on the interpretation of the features as a Roman road. Parchmarks (*see page* 27) subsequently allowed the line of the road to be easily distinguished from the former field boundaries.

The western part of this alignment, to the west of the B4547, survives in places as a spread and somewhat fragmentary *agger* running though a boggy area in improved pasture. It is, in places, defined by an area free of rushes, indicating better drainage. At one point the *agger* appears to have been built up to cross a natural hollow and is still approximately 8m wide at its base.

31 Photograph provided by the Central Register of Aerial Photography for Wales. Ref. Snowdonia National Park 2/10/86 5186149
32 Photograph provided by the Central Register of Aerial Photography for Wales. Ref. SNP 2/10/86 5186165
33 Evans H, 1966 'Llanddeiniolen Rectory', *Archaeology in Wales* p.9
34 note: Llys Dinorddwig is referred to in Pennant, 1770, *A Tour in Wales* Vol.II, p.167
35 RCAHMW, 1960. *An Inventory of Ancient Monuments in Caernarvonshire* Vol.II, p.lxiii
36 Central Register of Aerial Photography for Wales Ref. SNP 3/10/86 5286041

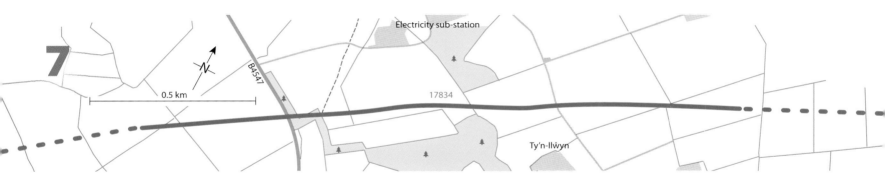

7

Electricity sub-station

B4547

0.5 km

17834

Ty'n-llŵyn

The road to the east of the B4547 initially runs through woodlands and has been adopted by a more recent track, shown on the 1832 Vaynol estate map, running as far as the long-abandoned Dinorwic Tramway. It is again visible beyond the former tramway as a low *agger*, roughly 5m wide. This runs through a modern gate and has been adopted by a later track which is shown on the 1889 25" OS map as a footpath leading to Ty'n-llwyn. These later improvements seem to have added to the Roman road as opposed to replacing it; it is still 5m wide and raised above the surrounding ground level. Its character abruptly changes where it turns to the west and runs across a particularly boggy area, becoming well-defined, flat-topped, and bounded by a wall and a ditch. This is probably exclusively post-Roman and part of the later path, marking the point where it leaves the line of the

Roman road and turns towards Ty'n-llwyn. The crop mark is very clear in the fields to the north of Ty'n-Llwyn (*photograph below*). These have been regularly ploughed and the road does not survive as an earthwork. This is the last stretch of road that has been identified with any certainty on the coastal plain. Several suggestions have been made and several linear crop marks caused by pipelines have added to the confusion. A linear bank close to Tynyffridd **SH58126827** could be significant; it looks like a Roman road from the air[37] but appeared to be a field bank when examined on the ground. Richard Fenton records in his *Tours of Wales* in 1810 that a milestone was found near Tŷ Coch, Pentir, during clearance of Cyttiau'r Gwyddelod ('Irishman's huts', i.e. hut circles) from a cornfield above the house. It was found in 1806, but was lost by 1846 and hasn't been seen since. As with the stone

from near Llys Dinorwig, it appears to have been found in a Romano-British hut group and therefore had been moved from its original position. In this case it would have been about 1.2km north of the projected line of the road.

Margary projects a line from Tŷ Coch to Abergwyn-gregyn mainly following the line of hedgerows and lanes, but there is no evidence on the ground until it reaches the site of a milestone **SH66887338** at Madryn Farm. The road turns inland at this point, and two milestones found at Gorddinog indicate its approximate line as it climbs into the uplands. A replica of one of the milestones stands at its find-spot (*see page 4*). The road then crosses to the Conwy Valley via Bwlch y Ddeufaen (pass of the two stones), named after two prehistoric standing stones towards its north-east end. This pass is an important part of the east-west route that runs close to the north Wales coastline.

The general route has been used throughout recorded history, from the Roman road until the modern A55 dual carriageway and railway, because it avoids the uplands of Snowdonia. There is however a major obstacle where the

Parchmark of the Roman road near Pentir, 2013, PRN 17834

north-eastern end of the Snowdonia uplands terminates in two head-lands, Penmaen Mawr and Penmaen Bach. Both are steep and rocky with precipitous cliffs above the sea and they are now crossed using modern engineering in the form of tunnels and rock-cut terraces. Up until the eighteenth century travellers were forced to turn inland and use a more easily-traversed pass. Bwlch y Ddeufaen appears to have been the most commonly used route, leading to a crossing point of a second obstacle, the river Conwy. The route is flanked by a series of prehistoric monuments and so appears to be a truly ancient trackway. It therefore seems that the pass has been used almost continuously for well over 2,000 years. This has, unsurprisingly, left a profusion of hollow ways, tracks and roads making it very difficult to differentiate the Roman road from the other remains. The multi-period trackways are however fairly well-preserved, because the route was largely abandoned in the eighteenth century.

At this time, there was an attempt to build a turnpike road across the pass. This was, however, aborted and a road through the Sychnant pass was constructed instead.[38] In more recent times electricity pylons were constructed along the line of the old road and a narrow maintenance track was built. This has been upgraded in the last few years, probably obliterating some of the features recorded in the earlier accounts of the route. A major gas pipeline and a smaller pipe have produced two well-aligned linear features that run close to the line of the old road and have confused some investigators.

Several descriptions have been written of the Roman road across Bwlch y Ddeufaen. Bezant-Lowe recorded lengths of a paved road, 6ft wide.[39] RCAHMW and the OS investigators record lengths of shelves and banks along with fragments of paving. F K Bush of the OS field investigation team concluded, however, that 'the only extant portions of this road lie between **SH732715** and **SH720716**, where an *agger* is visible parallel to the modern road for short stretches'.[40] This is the most obvious length at the north-east end of the pass; the published descriptions suggested that there should be more extant road than this. A thorough investigation using aerial photographs and detailed field work was therefore undertaken as part of the current project.

Even a cursory examination of modern aerial photographs show that most of the multi-period trackways run in a very direct line across the pass with only the more recent access tracks picking a meandering route through the terrain. This is almost certainly because the earlier trackways follow the line of the Roman road, probably the only properly surveyed and engineered road to have been built along the route.

Aerial photographs of the pass taken in 1948 show it before the construction of the modern track, pipelines and pylons.[41] Most of the roads and trackways on the photographs still exist but the lack of modern features emphasises the direct route it takes across the uplands. The Roman Roads Project examined the route across the whole of the pass. The milestones at the south-eastern end (*see pages 5 and 27*) provide obvious points of reference; the first was found in 1959, 450m east-south-east of Madryn farm, and dates from AD261-262. It was however broken and had been set upside down and re-used as an early medieval memorial stone. This had therefore probably been moved. The other two stones were found close together in 1883 in a field at the top of the steep slope from the coastal plain. One dates from AD121-122 and states that it is eight Roman miles from Kanovium, the second dates from AD198-209. The route from the coastal plain to the uplands is not clear. The most obvious route would seem to be up Nant y Felin-fach close to the two milestones. Two tracks, one modern and an older track, were sectioned by William Halhed. Both were found to be less than 2.5m wide and do not appear to be of Roman character.[42]

ROMAN MILES
The mille passum *(Latin for 'a thousand paces' – in which each pace represents two steps), became known as the 'Roman mile'. It is estimated to measure about 1,479 metres, 0.92 of the modern-day mile of 1,609 metres.*

37 Photograph provided by the Central Register of Aerial Photography for Wales. Ref SNP 3/10/86 5286112
38 Dodd AH, 1925. 'The Roads of North Wales, 1750 to 1850', *Arch Camb* LXXX Pt.1 pp.130 and 132
39 Bezant Lowe W, 1927. *The Heart of Northern Wales* Vol.II, pp.132-4
40 RCAHMW, 1956. *An Inventory of Ancient Monuments in Caernarvonshire* Vol.I, p.lxxii / Ordnance Survey linear file RR67C 1971 NMR Aberystwyth
41 RAF 1948 CPE/UK2525 4058-62 and 4058-62 4040-42
42 Halhed WB, 1912. 'Roman Roads in North Wales, II' *Arch Camb* XII Pt.3 p.320

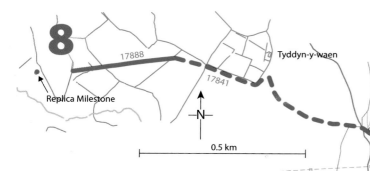

wall on the edge of the terrace. He also notes that Mr Richard Williams of Hengae stated that his grandfather could remember a roadside wall being built from stones taken from the Roman road.

The terrace, at its eastern end, runs alongside the modern track. The field-wall eventually turns to the north-east and the remains of the *agger* and hollow ways continue in a straight line from the line of the wall and terrace. **PRN 17572**. This demonstrates that the wall was

The line of the road across the pass is shown on **Map 8**; the relevant PRNs are noted in the text. The first part of the road after the climb from the uplands has only recently been discovered. A low bank **PRN 17888** running diagonally beneath early (probably medieval) field banks was noticed on an RCAHMW aerial photograph by Hugh Toller (*photograph right*). It is visible on the ground as a very low earthwork and is almost certainly the *agger* of the Roman road. This shows that the road runs towards the north side of the pass. This ties in well with Bezant-Lowe's account of the road from the 1920s. Both he and the RCAHMW record that the road runs along a shelf with a modern drystone wall running along its eastern edge (*photograph opposite, top*). This is still clearly visible **PRN 17571**; the wall runs along the outside of a 5m wide, well-defined terrace for 950m. Quarry pits are visible on the slope above, set back slightly from the road. Bezant-Lowe records that a paved road 6ft wide was found by excavation, with a surface of small flat stones, in some parts quite closely fitted together. He states that larger flat stones may have been the foundation and the thickness of surface was from 8cm to 15cm. This is considerably narrower than the existing terrace so it is unclear what he was looking at, perhaps a later phase. It also seems unlikely that the full width of the road was excavated, given the presence of the drystone

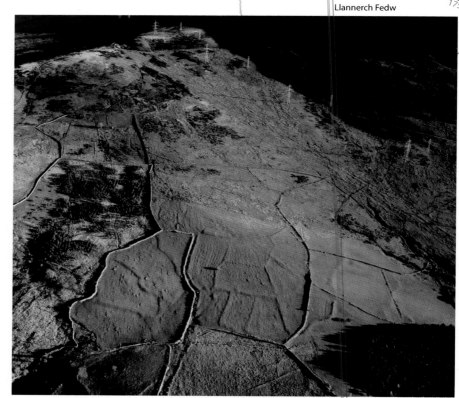

The line of the Roman road at the west end of Bwlch y Ddeufaen (PRN 17888). It is the bank diagonally crossing the old field boundaries in the foreground. (RCAHMW AP-2005-2849)

An unusual upland parchmark at the southern end of PRN 17691 near Rhiw Bach quarry

A trench across the road above Penamnen (PRN 17691). The road runs from left to right. The gravel surface has been removed on the right to expose the foundation slabs

ditches was cleared and a 5.5m wide, roughly-paved surface was exposed. This had been buried beneath about 0.6m of peat. The upland bogs in this area contain peat that is several metres deep and it was an easy task to locate the continuation of the road by probing; a 5m-wide hard surface was encountered at a depth of between 0.5 and 1m, (usually about 0.6m). On either side of this the probe could be pushed in to its full length of 1.3m indicating soft peat. This was traced for 1.05km from the east side of the head of Cwm Penamnen to the exposure above Rhiw Bach. **PRN 17691**. At the southern end the road was also clearly visible as a parch-mark; the stones beneath the peat were affecting the drainage causing the vegetation to be a different colour (*photograph above*).

The rough paving recorded in all of the ditches did not seem to be a typical Roman road; further investigation was clearly necessary, so a trial excavation was cut across the road in 2006. This revealed a very well-preserved 5.5m wide road beneath about 0.7m of peat.

The slate slabs were a foundation layer, laid directly onto the peat

or perhaps the original ground surface, acting as a raft to stop the road sinking into the soft ground. The usual construction techniques were not used here because there was a further 1.2m of peat beneath the road and therefore no solid substrate on which to build the *agger*. The slabs were covered with a typical surface of packed gravel and small stones in a silty clay matrix. Shallow roadside ditches, defined by a thin layer of silt in the peat, were faintly visible on either side. The whole construction was relatively slight with a total depth of no more than 0.18m.

53 Hall JP, 1923. *Caer Llugwy: excavation of the Roman fort between Capel Curig and Betws-y-Coed* pp.60-64

54 Margary, 1967 p.354

55 Waddelove E, 1999. *The Roman Roads of North Wales, Recent Discoveries* pp.127-9

56 Hopewell D, 2008. 'A470 Blaenau Ffestiniog and Cancoed Road Improvements: Archaeological Recording', *Archaeology in Wales* 48 pp.57-62

57 Bowen EG & Gresham C, 1967. *History of Merioneth* Vol.1, pp.246-8

58 Jones WT, Information deposited in Gwynedd HER regarding ongoing work by Dolwyddelan Historical Society

59 Crew P, 1980. 'Sarn Helen (Margary 69), Penmachno (SH738469)' in 'Roman Britain in 1979, 1: Sites Explored', by Grew F O, *Britannia* XI p.346 / Crew P, 1979 'Sarn Helen, Penmachno' Archaeology in Wales 19 p.28

Section across the excavated road

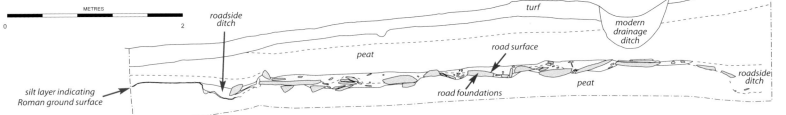

METRES

0   2

roadside ditch

turf

modern drainage ditch

peat

road surface

silt layer indicating Roman ground surface

road foundations

peat

roadside ditch

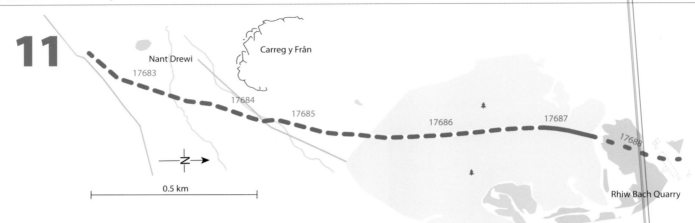

The road was flat-topped, perhaps even slightly concave, with a slight slope to the east, ensuring run-off into the lower ditch. This variation from the usual convex *agger* may have been a feature of the original design, but cracks in the peat beneath the road indicate that there had been shrinkage due to drying, so subsidence would also have been a factor in the eventual profile of the road. The surface was slightly thinner in the centre of the road, indicating a small amount of erosion. There were, however, no obvious signs of resurfacing apart from the possible infilling of a pot-hole. This suggests that the road was not heavily used, even during the Roman period, and went out of use soon after the forts at either end were abandoned. Patches of preserved long grass were found on top of the stones; this was presumably the first vegetation to colonise the abandoned road surface. The bottom part of a wooden Roman surveyor's peg was also found, preserved in the peat beneath edge of the road. (*See photograph on page 10.*) The raw materials for the road appear to have come from higher ground over 100m to the east. Here slabs have been levered off outcroppings of slate bedrock and scattered quarry pits can be seen where the peat cover is thinner. A peat column was extracted during the excavation and three preliminary radiocarbon dates were taken.[60] Peat from just above the road produced a date of AD610 to 780 confirming that the road was covered with peat soon after the Roman period.

The southward continuation of the road is cut by Rhiw Bach quarry but can then be traced for a further 5km across the uplands to just beyond Beddau Gwŷr Ardudwy **Maps 11 and 12** with a high degree of certainty. The line of the road was clearly used in post-Roman times and post-medieval improvements have hidden or modified parts of the original earthwork but enough survives to enable the route to

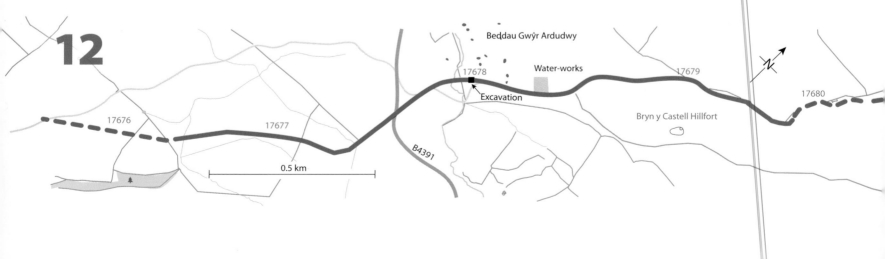

be traced in detail. Fragments of agger, terraces and quarry pits all provide evidence for its origins. Excavations by Gwynedd Archaeological Trust at Beddau Gwŷr Ardudwy in 1990 confirmed that the modern road overlies the eroded Roman earthwork.[61] **PRN 17678**.

The line of the road is briefly lost as it crosses the Cynfal valley but is again preserved as an *agger* crossing rough moorland just to the north of Tomen y Mur. **Map 13**, **PRN 17671-2**. The preserved parts of this route are a good example of an upland Roman road in Wales. It crosses some of the most inhospitable uplands in Gwynedd but maintains a direct line albeit with adjustments to avoid obstacles.

The old trackway 1.4 km to the north of Beddau Gwŷr Ardudwy shows some signs of later engineering but follows the direct line of the Roman road

60 Peat from a little below the road gave a date of 2100+/-40 BP (2 sigma calibration Cal BC 340 to 330 and Cal BC 200 to 30), peat from a little above the road gave a date of 1340+/-60 BP (2 sigma calibration Cal AD610 to 780) and organic sediment towards the base of the peat produced a date of 7760+/- 60 BP (Cal BC 6690 to 6470) Information from Astrid Castledine.

61 Longley D, 1996. 'Archaeological Survey and Excavation near Ffestiniog and Gellilydan', *Journal of the Merioneth Historical and Record Society* XII pp.211-220.

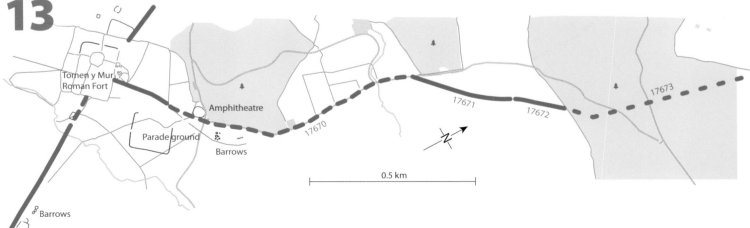

13

Road RR68 part 1
Segontium — Tomen y Mur

Map 2
page 24

The evidence for this road is sparse, with little or no evidence on the ground. Routes have been proposed and published but all fall short of proving the route. Margary traces the road between Segontium and Croesor along current roads and a 'terrace lane high on the west slopes between Rhyd-ddu and Beddgelert'.[62] The course of the terrace lane could not, however, be determined by the OS investigators.[63] The route between Croesor and the vale of Ffestiniog is described by Bowen & Gresham.[64] This follows the line of the old coach road and an earlier pack horse trail. Again no surviving Roman road was identified by the OS surveyors.

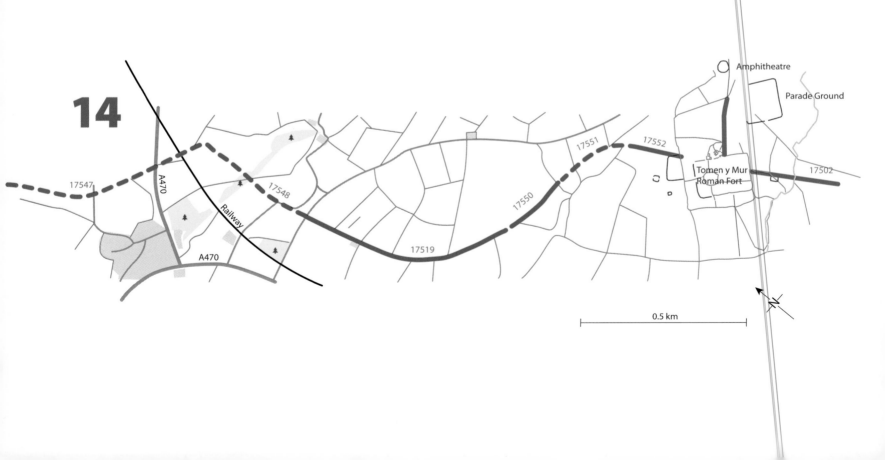

14

0.5 km

The remaining 3.5km between the Vale of Ffestiniog and Tomen y Mur follows various tracks and roads and can be followed as terraces and an *agger* for about 1km before the fort.[65] The route from the crossing of the Afon Dwyrd was assessed during the Roman Roads Project. **Map 14**. A road can be followed for 2.5km, mostly as a terrace through improved pasture. It has been adopted by post-medieval tracks for much of its length and has been partly truncated as it approaches the recently improved A470. This route can be seen to be earlier than the roads crossing it, but little remains to prove its Roman origins.

The line of the road is fairly certain from the point where it crosses the minor road to Tomen y Mur 200m from the A470 **PRN 17549-50** although it should be noted that this could also be interpreted as being part of RRX95 (*page 57*). Initially it is largely destroyed by a deeply-cut modern lane leading to an old barn. A further 50m length of road has been recently disturbed by the construction of a new barn. This, however, had the advantage of exposing a longitudinal section through the *agger*. The metalling consists of small stones, gravel and clay and is 10-15cm thick. The body of the *agger* appears to be about 25cm thick and built up out of clay subsoil. The original ground surface was not visible but the *agger* appeared to be stonier than the undisturbed subsoil. The road to the south and east of this is generally well preserved. It is initially visible as a 5.5m wide *agger* running through improved pasture and then as a 5m wide terrace alongside a stream. There has been serious erosion in places where the stream has meandered and cut into the road. The terrace is best preserved in **PRN 17550**.

After this point the road passes through improved pasture and is barely visible, except for an oblique hollow running to the corner of the fort. **PRN 17552**. This has been accepted as Roman by Bowen and Gresham and the OS, but seems to be anomalous as it does not run to a gate. This may belong to a later phase, perhaps associated with the medieval re-use of the fort.

The line of most of this road is 'predicted' and therefore unproven. It could be argued that the road may just be an invention of archaeologists. There is good evidence for an alternative route to the west, RRX95, via the fort at Pen Llystyn (Bryncir) making the route of RR68 functionally unnecessary as a linking road. It is also unusually long at 34km, considerably more than a standard day's march. The only good evidence is on the approaches to Tomen y Mur and this could alternatively be interpreted as being part of the road from Pen Llystyn. The route may have been important as an access point into the upland region as opposed to a simple link between the forts but further physical evidence is needed before it can be accepted as a proven route.

62 Margary, 1967 pp.351-2

63 OS linear files RR 68 1973

64 Bowen EG & Gresham C, 1967. *History of Merioneth* Vol.1, pp.256-8

65 Bowen & Gresham and OS *ibid*.

Road RR68 part 2
Tomen y Mur — Caer Gai

Map 3
page 25

The road running south-east from Tomen y Mur is, on current evidence, the most complete Roman road in Gwynedd. The route was first traced in detail by Colonel H C Irvine and published in the *Bulletin of the Board of Celtic Studies* in 1956.[66] Much of his proposed route was dismissed by the Ordnance Survey surveyors in 1973 and the RCAHMW also considered it unproven.[67] In contrast, recent work on this route by Crew & Musson, Kelly and the Roman Roads Project in 2003/4 have shown Irvine's work to be one of the more accurate published accounts of a Roman road in Wales.[68]

The road to the east of Tomen y Mur can be traced as an earthwork for 5.3km. **Map 15**. The road leaves the south-east gate of the fort, where bridge abutments followed by a ploughed out *agger* can be seen **PRN 17502-3**, before two alignments appear skirting a burial mound. **PRNs 17503 and 17511**.

It had been assumed that the road then followed a modern track **PRN 17505**, but an aerial photograph taken by Toby Driver for RCAHMW[69] shows that the road runs as a terrace through improved pasture further to the south. It is then overlaid by modern tracks **PRN 17506-7** but still retains the characteristic Roman quarry pits as far as the Afon Llafar at Dolddinas.

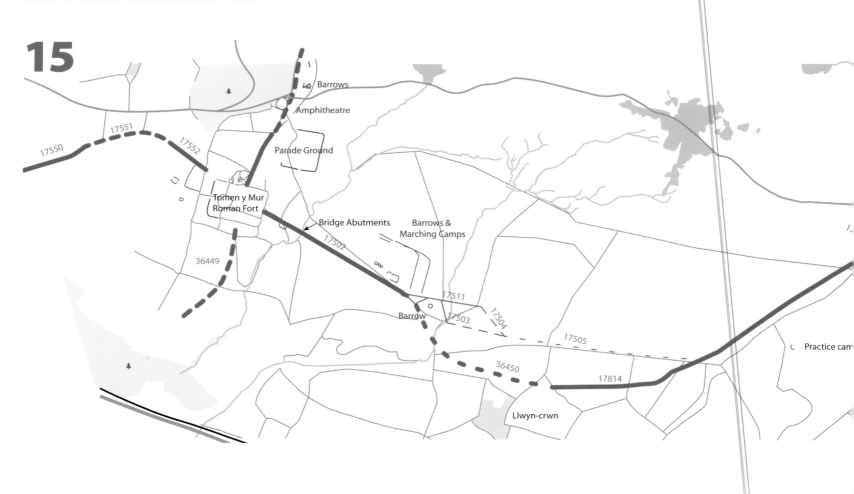

The Roman road to the east of Tomen y Mur, PRN 17814.
The quarry pits above the road at the top right are particularly clear. (RCAHMW AP-2005-2970)

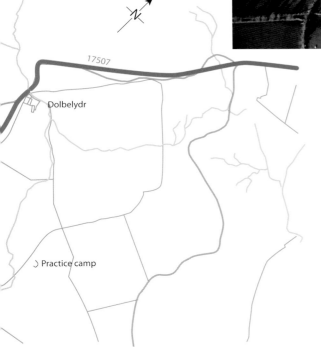

0.5 km

17507

Dolbelydr

Practice camp

66 Irvine HC, 1956. 'Note on the Roman Road between Caer Gai and Tomen y Mur',
Bulletin of the Board of Celtic Studies XVII Pt.1 pp.57-68

67 OS linear files RR68 1973 / RCAHMW, 1964. *An Inventory of Ancient Monuments
in Caernarvonshire* Vol.III, p.lxxxiv

68 Crew P & Musson C, 1996. *Snowdonia from the Air, Patterns in the Landscape* p.30
/ Kelly RS, 1986. 'A section across the road between Caer Gai and Tomen y Mur',
JMHRS X Pt.II pp.169-171

69 2005-2970 PRN 17814

The route can then be traced as an almost undisturbed series of terraces and lengths of *agger* across the uplands to the south-west of Llyn Hiraethllyn and down the slope to Cwm Prysor. **Map 16, PRN 17509-10.** The road near the lake runs around the edge of bogs and is unusually narrow, little more than 3m wide.

The road approaching Cwm Prysor is illustrated particularly well by an aerial photograph by Crew & Musson. This shows a distinctive zigzag running down the steep slope along with diagnostic quarry pits on both sides of the road. Environment Agency lidar survey for this area also shows the road and quarry pits and allows the line to be traced beyond the aerial photographic evidence. The road runs obliquely across the valley bottom before joining a modern farm track.[70]

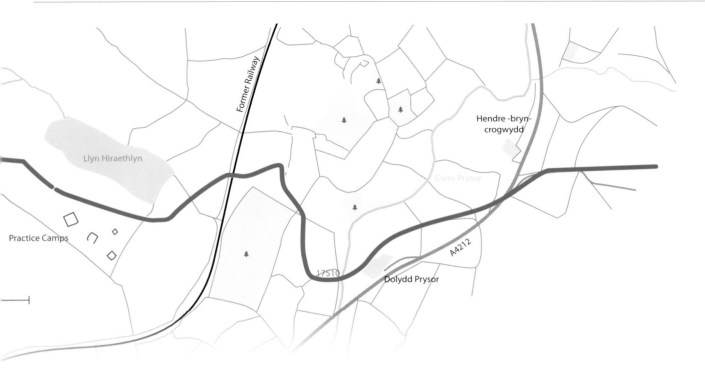

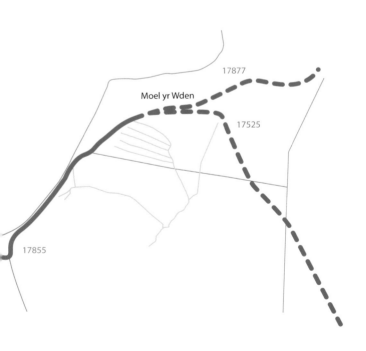

This joins neatly to a zigzag running up the east side of the valley that was discovered in the 2006 season of the Roman Roads Project. The zigzag is somewhat eroded and has been used as a fairly recent access to the uplands, possibly during twentieth century military exercises. This leads to a well preserved *agger* at the top of the slope, with associated quarry pits. **Map 17**, **PRN 17855**.

The route is well preserved as it climbs to Moel yr Wden.

70 Information from Hugh Toller

Colonel Irvine's proposed route across Cwm Prysor runs further to the north, and in the light of current evidence is almost certainly incorrect. His route through the uplands to the east of Prysor, below Moel y Slates, is almost certainly correct. The road initially runs across featureless bogs and can be seen as a low agger and a change in vegetation and then as a slight earthwork within a fire-break in commercial forestry. **Map 18, PRNs 17875 and 17524.**

The Roman character of this route was confirmed by Richard Kelly during an excavation to investigate the feature before the planting of the forest at Blaen-lliw-uchaf in 1986.[71] He cut a section across the road revealing a 4.25m wide *agger* with a surface of angular stones in a matrix of clayey soil. This was flanked by shallow side ditches.

The road to the east of Prysor is particularly hard to find. Here it is a slightly terraced agger accentuated by a change in vegetation.

18

0.5 km

Moel y Slates

17524

17875

17876

17877

Moel yr Wden

17525

Bwlch y Bi

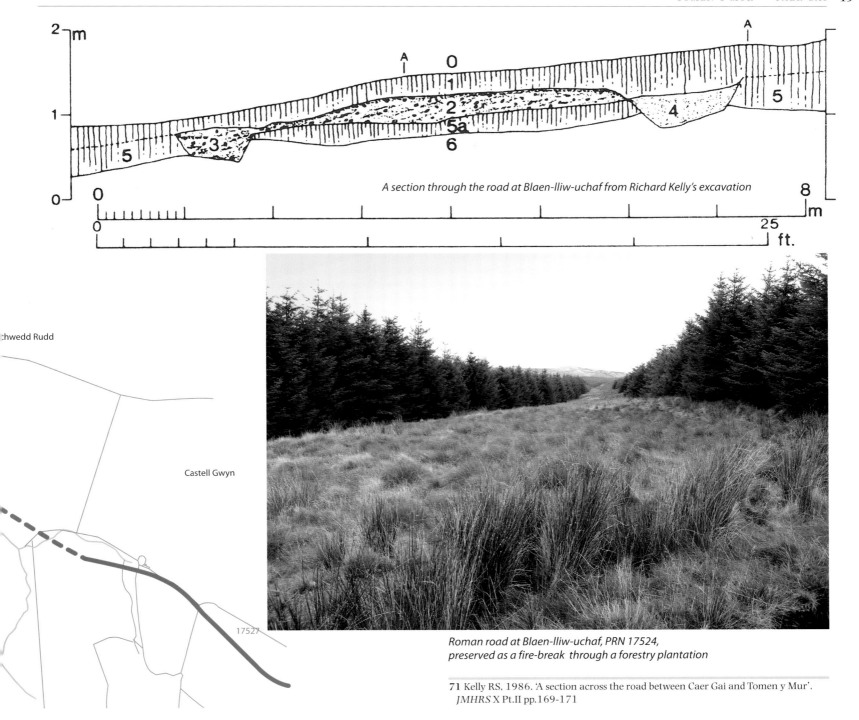

A section through the road at Blaen-lliw-uchaf from Richard Kelly's excavation

chwedd Rudd

Castell Gwyn

17527

Roman road at Blaen-lliw-uchaf, PRN 17524,
preserved as a fire-break through a forestry plantation

71 Kelly RS, 1986. 'A section across the road between Caer Gai and Tomen y Mur'.
JMHRS X Pt.II pp.169-171

Much of Irvine's route to the west and south-east of Moel y Slates was dismissed by the OS surveyors. It is not easy to find amongst the rough tussocky grass of the boggy moorland, but with perseverance and good light it is possible to trace most of the 4.7km of road from Moel yr Wden to Foel Ystrodur Bach. A series of *aggeres*, terraces and cuttings, 4.5 to 5m wide, take a fairly direct route across the open moorland. It is even blocked by a short length of relatively recent field wall, demonstrating at least some continuity of use. **Maps 18 to 19, PRNs 17526-7 and 17807-8.** Interestingly, there are few of the braided hollow ways and large areas of erosion that are often found on multi-period mountain passes. This gives the impression that the route was not used to any great extent after the Roman period. An early abandonment is also suggested by the excavated section, that showed little evidence of wear to the road surface, and by accumulations of peat, up to 50cm deep, over parts of the road.

A later track overlies the Roman road just to the north of Bryn Cau and runs towards Ffridd Trawscoed. The presence of quarry pits shows that this is a continuation of the Roman alignment even though the track is clearly a modern construction. **PRN 17528.**

Two alternative routes have been suggested for the eastern part of this road, one along the Lliw Valley by Archdeacon Thomas and one through Y Lordship by Barri Jones.[72] The OS surveyors failed to find any confirming evidence for either route. A parch mark **Map 28, PRN 17809** (*see page* 70) visible on an aerial photograph taken by Hugh Toller in 1989 and also visible as a low earthwork on Environment Agency lidar survey, shows a road running from the end of the avenue to the west of Caer Gai along the Lliw valley. This may provide a link, running up Nant Eglwysarn to the uplands. The *sarn* (causeway) element of the place name may also be significant. Peter Crew suggests that there may be a side road **Map 18, PRN 17525** running to kilns at Bwlch y Bi. This is clearly not a major military road as it is barely 2m wide in places, but it may be a Roman packhorse trail connecting the kilns and the main Roman road.[73]

Most of road RR68pt2 can now be traced with a high degree of certainty. Much of the road to the east of Cwm Prysor is in open access land and makes an interesting walk along the line of one of the most remote roads in the region. It is, however, also a good example of a road that is very hard to trace. The use of a detailed map and a hand held GPS is recommended on this route.

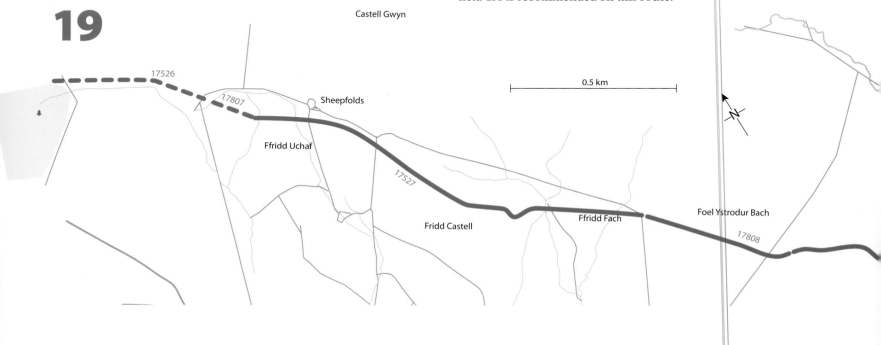

19

Castell Gwyn

17526

17807

Sheepfolds

Ffridd Uchaf

0.5 km

17527

N

Fridd Castell

Ffridd Fach

Foel Ystrodur Bach

17808

*The unusual post-medieval dry stone wall
blocking the Roman road at Ffridd Uchaf*

Fridd Trawsgoed

17528

Afon Erwent

17528

17528

n Cau

72 Thomas DR, 1885. 'The Roman Station of Caergai', *Arch Camb* Vol.II VII p.199
/ Jones GDB, 1959. 'Roman Merionethshire: The Roman Road West of Caer Gai',
BBCS XVIII Pt.II p.214 footnote

73 Crew P, 1979. 'Craig y Ffolt, Llanuwchllyn', *Arch in Wales* 19 p.55

Road RRX95 part 1
Segontium — Pen Llystyn

Map 2
page 24

As we have seen, there is little proof for RR68, from Segontium to Tomen y Mur via the Aberglaslyn Pass and Maentwrog. The discovery of a fort at Pen Llystyn in 1959 showed that there was a more westerly route linking the two forts, which avoided the treacherous terrain of the uplands.[74] The first part of this route, from Segontium to Pen Llystyn, passes through easily-traversable land that skirts the higher ground. Most of this is improved agricultural land and until recently there was no indication of the line of the Roman road.

A probable line has now been found for several kilometres using modern technology and communications. The main discovery was made using online data by Bryn Gethin, an archaeologist from Warwickshire, who spotted a series of long, straight archaeological features on the Environment Agency lidar images. **Maps 20 to 22.** The discovery was then circulated and discussed via e-mail with Hugh Toller in London and Gwynedd Archaeological Trust in Wales. Hugh Toller showed that a possible *agger* was visible in a few places on Google Earth aerial photographs from 2010. This was followed up by fieldwork by Hugh, John Burman and Gwynedd Archaeological Trust; a truly modern collaborative project.

As noted earlier in the book, lidar is an effective tool for discovering and mapping Roman roads (*see page 14*). The standard resolution Environment Agency data consists of measurements taken every metre with a vertical accuracy of about 15cm. This is not particularly useful for the detection of small earthworks but larger features, even if they are very low, show up clearly. Of course, linear features discovered in this way need to be examined on the ground in order to exclude modern features. The most convincing aspect of the features found on this route is that they can be seen to run for many kilometres, cutting across modern field systems, roads and villages in a way that suggests that they had fallen out of use and had mostly been forgotten by the time that current settlement patterns were being established. Fieldwork soon established that they were not pipelines or other modern features and therefore seemed to be archaeological features. They were, however, very difficult to see in the field. Lidar produces a ground model that 'sees through' most vegetation and has artificial illumination from one direction. This is similar to looking at a field with short grass on the evening of a sunny day, when every hump and bump is shown by the shadows cast by the low-angled light. These ideal conditions are unlikely to occur when carrying out fieldwork; grass and vegetation is often long and uneven, the sun may not be shining and it is certainly beyond the power of an archaeologist to get it to shine in the right direction and at the right angle.

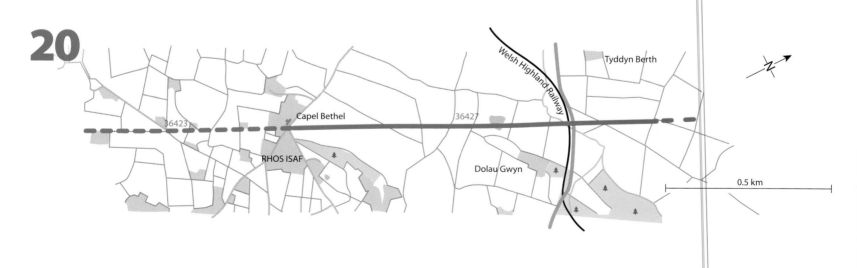

Field visits were made to many of the accessible lengths of the possible road, some were visible but several were in long grass or were too low and indistinct to be seen in flat light.

The most northerly part of the road that has so far been identified **Map 20, PRN 36427** (*see the lidar image, right*) is about 4km from Segontium on an alignment running to the east of the fort, presumably in order to avoid the steep-sided part of the Afon Gwyrfai, and leading from a crossing near Cae-mawr. It runs in a dead straight line for 1.1km from just north of the Welsh Highland Railway near Tyddyn Berth, to Capel Bethel at Rhos Isaf. At the north it is visible as a 5m wide spread *agger* and can be seen on aerial photographs further to the south.

The line of the Roman road south of Caernarfon (PRN 36427) is visible on the Environment Agency lidar survey as a straight feature cutting across the line of almost all later development

Environment Agency lidar composite 2012

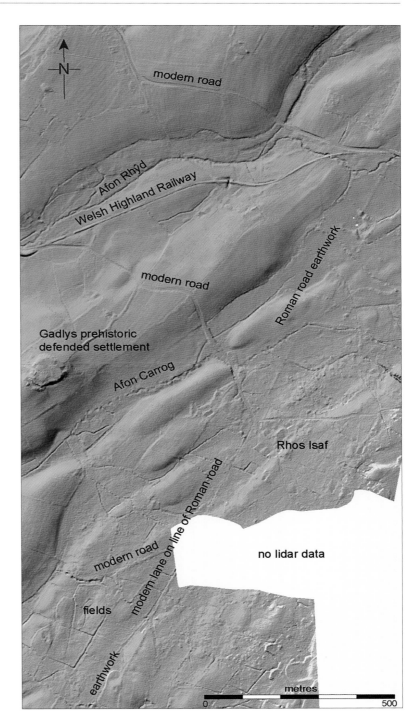

74 Hogg AHA, 1969. 'Pen Llystyn: A Roman Fort and other remains', *Archaeological Journal* 125, pp.101-92

The line is adopted by a modern road for 0.6km before again becoming visible on Environment Agency lidar for 0.7km between Gilwern-isaf and Bryn Goleu. **Map 21, PRN 36429**. After a short stretch of modern road, it can be again traced on lidar and is just about visible on the ground as an intermittent low *agger* for 0.4m to the east of Groeslon. **PRN 36431**. There is a break in the lidar coverage to the south of this.

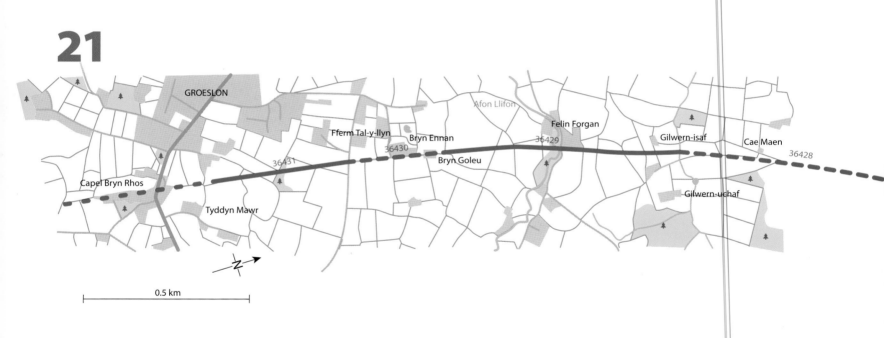

21

GROESLON

Afon Llifon

Felin Forgan

Fferm Tal-y-llyn

Bryn Ennan

Gilwern-isaf

Cae Maen

36430

36429

36428

Bryn Goleu

36431

Capel Bryn Rhos

Gilwern-uchaf

Tyddyn Mawr

N

0.5 km

One further length can be seen intermittently on lidar to the south of Penygroes on a similar line to that proposed by Waddelove.[75] **Map 22, PRN 36433**. It appears that Ffordd-y-Brenin in the east of the village runs along the line of the Roman road. The line can be followed for 1.6km to Llwdcoed beyond which there is nothing else is visible. It seems likely that a minor road follows the line of the Roman road from close to Pennant Bach for 5km to Dafarn Faig, just to the north of the site of Pen Llystyn fort. The Roman road can then be seen on lidar, emerging from beneath the A487 and running for a short distance to the site of the fort.

In conclusion, the identification of these low earthworks as Roman roads in not absolutely proven: a programme of trial excavation would be needed to conclusively identify Roman features. They are almost certainly early; they predate most of the current settlement and field patterns, which probably have medieval to eighteenth century origins. They are running close to the predicted line of the Roman road and have a typical direct, linear, Roman form. It is therefore difficult to provide an alternative explanation for their origins and their identification as Roman roads must be fairly secure.

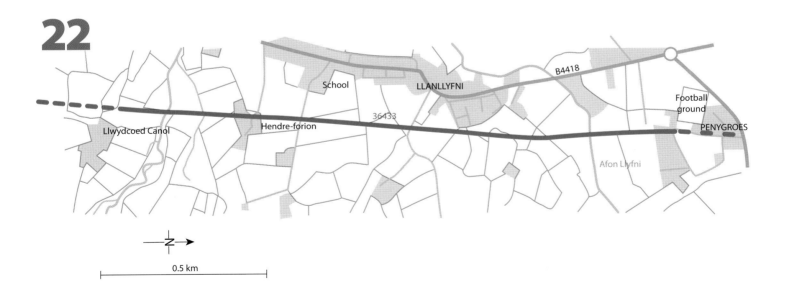

22

School
B4418
LLANLLYFNI
Football ground
36433
PENYGROES
Llwydcoed Canol
Hendre-forion
Afon Llyfni

N

0.5 km

75 Waddelove E, 1999. *The Roman Roads of North Wales, Recent Discoveries* pp.228-232

Map 2
page 24

Road RRX95 part 2
Pen Llystyn — Tomen y Mur

The road from Pen Llystyn to Tomen y Mur remains elusive. Routes have been proposed by RCAHMW and the OS field investigation team.[76] These, for the most part, run along modern roads and tracks and no extant Roman features have been identified. A tenuous suggestion of an early road on this alignment was noted by RCAHMW. In the *Mabinogion* story of *Math fab Mathonwy*, the men from South Wales after their defeat by Math near Caernarfon, fell back along a route from Nant Coll to Maentwrog via Dolbenmaen and Traeth Mawr.

The only Roman features on the proposed line of the road are at Tremadog, where a Roman bath house, a corn drier, a lime-kiln and a stack of roofing slates have been identified[77] **SH55694012**. These may not be military structures but probably indicate roadside activity, The area to the west of the bath house around Llidiart Yspytty forms a narrow transport corridor. The road, if it followed the north side of Traeth Mawr, must have run along this 160m wide strip of land be-

tween the marshes and cliffs to the north. The area was examined during works in advance of the construction of a hospital on its northern part.

There was no surface indication of the Roman road, but the line of the pre-1845 Caernarvonshire Turnpike Trust road running along a terrace on the slopes above Traeth Mawr at **SH55504036** appeared to be the most likely route. A section was excavated across this, but all that remained was a terrace, cut into the subsoil with no signs of either metalling or an earlier phase.[78] The road terrace was revetted with post-medieval masonry. It therefore appears that any evidence for a Roman road on this alignment would have been destroyed by the turnpike.

The current landscape around Tremadog is largely artificial. An embankment known as the Cob was built across the mouth of the Glaslyn estuary in the early nineteenth century. The land behind this was then reclaimed producing the present regular fields and settlements. Previous to this the Traeth Mawr or Great Sands presented a serious obstacle to travel. This was a tidal estuary, containing a few islands, and could be treacherous. The traditional crossing point, before the marshes were drained, was between Llidiart Yspytty (the area around the bath house) and Minffordd. This is shown on Evans's 1797 Map of Wales. An interesting account is recorded in a letter from Mr Ellis Owen FSA[79] giving more information about this route (running from east to west) :

Opposite Felenrhyd is a ford to cross the Traeth Bach. At Penrhyndeudraeth is a farm called Tyddynisaf where a few years ago ... were found a great number (about two quarts) of Roman coins of Constantinus. ... The Minffordd fords are considered to be the best on Traeth Mawr, being harder, more shallow though broader, and very easily forded in the direction leading to Llidiart Yspytty (Hospital's Gate) to the west of Tremadoc with its Bryn y Fynwent where I myself have seen graves opened. ... Between Llidiart Yspytty and the village of Penmorfa are traces of a paved road.

Excavations at the Roman building at Glasfryn, Tremadog in 1908
(from Breese and Anwyl, 1909)

fort was never found and this was discounted with the discovery of the fortlet 4.5km to the east. Unfortunately this skews any early accounts of roads in this area. Secondly, the extensive forestry plantations of Coed y Brenin may have destroyed evidence. Thirdly the area contains lot of tracks and other disturbance produced by military exercises associated with the Second World War.

The first route was proposed by Margary and runs along the western side of Coed y Brenin and then along the modern road, via Llanelltyd, to Dolgellau. The 1889 OS 25" Map clearly shows the southern end of the *agger* at Pen-y-stryd **PRN 17736** turning to the west. This part of the road, in the triangle formed by two modern roads and the forestry plantation **PRNs 17853 and 17758**, has since been severely disturbed by the gas pipeline. However there is still a faint trace of a

Two straight features at Pen-y-stryd, PRN 17736 . On the left is the gas pipeline and on the right the parallel pair of ditches and agger of the Roman road

A view along the road near Pen-y-stryd. Members of a GAT guided walk are walking along the line of the road

feature, following the west turn shown on the OS map, on Environment Agency lidar. Beyond this point, the route follows the line of the turnpike road and no further proven Roman features have been identified. This is worth following for a couple of miles, although much of it is an upgraded track leading to the forests of Coed y Brenin. There are some well-preserved turnpike remains, particularly where the road first runs into the plantation.

Two phases are clearly visible where the road runs downhill just after entering the plantation. The earliest phase is, however, characteristically eighteenth century in character; an early surface of pitched-stone metalling can be seen joining the modern track at **SH72242922**. A particularly striking turnpike milestone survives a short distance into the forestry (*illustrated on page 16*). The only possible length of surviving Roman road is a length of eroded early road **SH72623134** that runs up the slope opposite Pen-y-stryd Chapel on a different alignment

93 Margary, 1967. pp.347-8 / Bowen & Gresham 1967. pp.247-53

94 Hugh Toller pers. com.

95 St Joseph JK, 1961. 'Air Reconnaissance in Britain, 1958-1960', *Journal of Roman Studies* 51 p.130

roughly parallel to the modern road. This predates the 1889 25" OS map which shows the modern road on its present alignment. The fact that it is the only earthwork emerging from the disturbance by roads and forestry at the end of Pen-y-stryd must mark it as a serious candidate for the Roman road. Beyond this, the turnpike and miles of forestry have made the chances of finding further Roman remains unlikely. This route is named as 'Sarn Helen' on Ordnance Survey maps.

The second route was proposed by Bowen and Gresham and follows a route to the east of Moel Hafod Owen via Abergeirw **SH76872896**. There are, on first inspection, several reasons for favouring Bowen and Gresham's route. These include possible extant fragments of road near Llech Idris **SH73203133** and at Bwlch Goriwared **SH76482456**; the position of an early Christian stone called 'Bedd Porus' **SH73303137** and another Roman tile kiln[96] **SH73103120** close to the road, and the

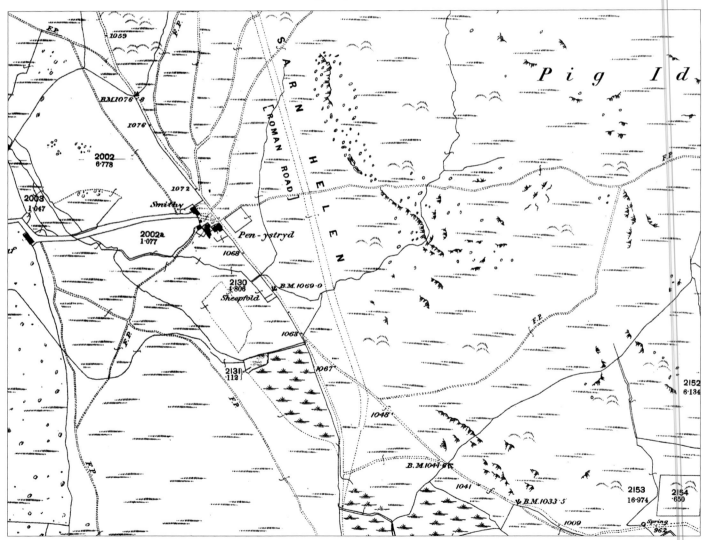

Road RR69b at Pen-y-stryd, from the 1889 25 inch Ordnance Survey map

road's alignment with the fortlet at Brithdir. On further examination the signs are less convincing. The road near Llech Idris is visible as a very faint 4m wide terrace that cannot be confirmed as Roman. The road through Bwlch Goriwared is a typical multi-period routeway consisting of braided hollow ways alongside a more modern track. No Roman engineering could be identified, despite a thorough search during a field visit in 2006. Elsewhere it seems unlikely that the Roman road follows the line of the present road, as suggested by Bowen and Gresham. It runs along some very steep slopes in a fashion atypical of Roman roads and there is no evidence of any earlier phases. Unless the modern road follows the Roman with absolutely no deviations there should be some extant road through the miles of unimproved land along the projected line. Finally the original position of the Bedd Porus stone is unknown. This route must therefore be considered unproven.

The third route was described in 1890 by Prys Morris in *Cantref Meirionydd: ei Chwedlau, ei Hynafiaeth, a'i Hanes* and has recently been examined in detail by Hugh Toller.[97] This road runs even further to the east than Bowen and Gresham's route. It mostly follows the current road from Pen-y-stryd as far as Abergeirw and then runs eastwards along the upper Mawddach valley, initially across improved pasture to the north of the river before crossing and following the modern road to Dolcynafon. There are fragments of an early road here but nothing that can be proven to be Roman.

The road to the east of Dolcynafon **Map 25, PRN 36440** then runs as a terrace, before describing a wide S-shaped zigzag and running southwards along the west side of Nant y Helig as far as a crossing point at **SH79792782**. It is a terrace between 3 and 5m wide but with obvious slippage from above, so was originally generally wider. Crucially it runs beneath a substantial boundary bank that is almost certainly the boundary of Cistercian lands and therefore early twelfth century.[98] This certainly adds credence to this route. The road then crosses the river and disappears into a forestry plantation. The 1899 25" OS map shows a continuation of the road, now mostly adopted by forestry tracks, in a direct line for a further 4km. Beyond this the road describes a large zigzag at **SH79562359** before running into cultivated land, where it could follow many different routes. The road can, however, be seen at this point to have made good topographical sense, despite its apparently circuitous route from Pen-y-stryd. It has bypassed the highlands of Rhobel Fawr and is aligned with RRN51 (see below), 4km to the south.

In some ways this latter road is the most convincing of the three routes, as it connects directly with the route going south and seems to have very early origins. It has, however, continued to be used since Roman times, albeit without being adopted by a turnpike. It therefore seems unlikely that much of it is unaltered Roman road. There is clearly potential for further research here, possibly enabling a conclusion to be made about a road that has puzzled researchers for over 200 years.

96 Crew P, 1990. 'Dolgain Trawsfynydd (SH731312)', *Archaeology in Wales* 30 pp.56-7

97 Toller H, 2008. 'The Roman road from Tomen y Mur towards Pennal', unpublished manuscript

98 Williams DH, 1990. *Atlas of Cistercian Lands in Wales* Map 14

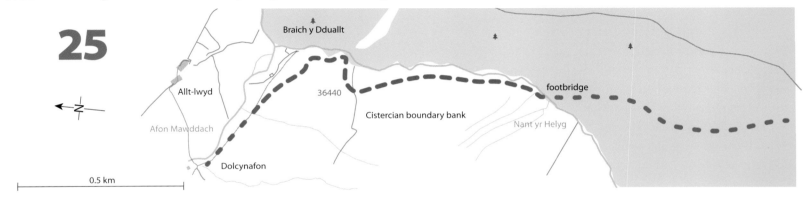

25

Braich y Dduallt

Allt-lwyd

36440

Afon Mawddach

Dolcynafon

Cistercian boundary bank

Nant yr Helyg

footbridge

0.5 km

Map 3
page 25

Roads RRN51 *and* RRN52
Brithdir Triangle

John Rigg and Hugh Toller[99] proposed a road from Brithdir to Long Mountain, but this was later retracted when it was realised that most of the recorded features were turnpike road (*see page 74*). Part of this route consisted of a link from RR66b to the east of Brithdir to RRX73 at the west end of Bwlch Oerddrws. Aerial photographic evidence has subsequently shown that there is little doubt that a Roman road, RRN51, runs along this 'link' route, even though much of it lies beneath the later turnpike. This was published in *Snowdonia from the Air* and is a superb example of the value of aerial photography in the study of Roman roads (*right*). The features are quite difficult to see on the ground but are very clear from the air.[100]

Most of this road is in open access land and is a good place to see the differences and similarities between turnpike roads and Roman roads. The easiest access to the road is from the north, down a track through forestry land **Map 26, PRN 17780** that starts between Tŷ Newydd Uchaf and Pont Helygog. There is little trace of Roman features as it passes through the woodland, but once it emerges onto the moorland beyond **PRN 17779**, quarry pits can be seen, set back a few metres from the edge of the road. The surface of the current track is a mixture of modern construction and turnpike road. An earthwork on top of a rise (62m to the north-west of the road, shortly after it leaves the forest) has been interpreted as a Roman signal station.[101]

The current track with its flanking Roman quarry pits can be traced for 1.2km. At a point where the road begins to swing to the east, to the north-east of the fields of Cae'r Tyddyn, there are no more quarry pits. This is where the turnpike and Roman road diverge. The turnpike swings away to the south-east **PRN 17777** in the form of a 3m wide terrace with stone revetting. There are still occasional quarry pits but these are immediately adjacent to the road unlike the Roman versions that are set back by a few metres and are much more frequent.

The Roman road and extensive quarry pits diverging from the more obvious turnpike road and running through the fields above Cae'r Tyddyn (RCAHMW 95-CS-0833)

The Roman road continues in a more southerly direction **PRN 17778** in the form of a 5m wide *agger* with some impressively large quarry pits to the west (*right*). This can be traced for 120m before it crosses into semi-improved farmland. Crew and Musson's aerial photograph shows faint traces of the road as it runs south through the fields to emerge on the current A470, just to the east of Cae'r Tyddyn. No further road has so far been traced on this alignment.

This is a curious length of road; there is little doubt that it is Roman, but it does not fit into our previous understanding of the road network in this area. The road neither runs to the fortlet at Brithdir, nor does it connect with most of the postulated alignments to the north and south, although the eastern alignment of RR69b, as traced by Prys Morris and later by Hugh Toller, is on this alignment. The lack of surviving road beyond the intersection with the A470 leaves open the possibilities of a route to the east over Bwlch Oerddrws, or perhaps a connection to the disputed route to Cefn Caer, Pennal, via Cross Foxes and Corris (RR66b) passing the newly discovered camp at Gwanas Fawr **Map 4** (*page 26*).[102] Rigg & Toller suggested the presence of a short cut, RRN52, to Brithdir **Map 25** (*page 63*); there is a rough track but it shows no signs of Roman military engineering.

Another GAT outing; standing in the middle of the road near Cae'r Tyddyn. A line of rushes defines the roadside ditch on the left

99 Rigg J & Toller H, 1983. 'A Roman Road from the Long Mountain to Dolgellau and Some Branches', *Britannia* XIV, p.11

100 Crew P & Musson C, 1996. *Snowdonia from the Air, Patterns in the Landscape* p.31

101 Burnham BC & Davies JL (eds), 2010. *Roman frontiers in Wales and the Marches* pp.300-301

102 Barker L, Burman J, Davies JL, Driver T, Hopewell D, Roberts JG & Toller H, 2007. 'A newly-discovered Roman camp at Gwanas Fawr, Brithdir and Llanfachreth, Gwynedd', *Archaeology in Wales* 47, pp.88-90

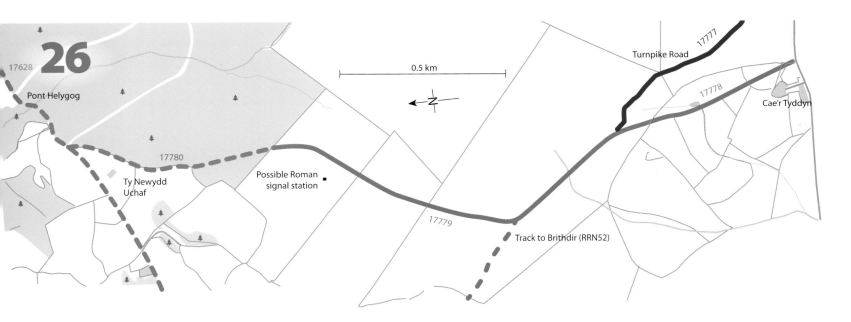

26

17628

Pont Helygog

0.5 km

N

Turnpike Road

17777

17778

Cae'r Tyddyn

17780

Ty Newydd Uchaf

Possible Roman signal station

17779

Track to Brithdir (RRN52)

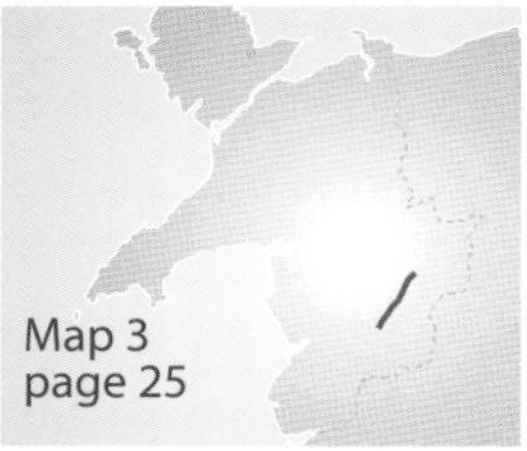

Map 3
page 25

Road RR66b
Caer Gai — Brithdir

This road appears to follow a fairly direct route between the two forts. It has been traced in detail by Jones and a similar, though not identical, route was proposed by Margary.[103] On leaving Caer Gai the road runs in a roughly south-westerly direction for about 4km, along modern roads and across open fields, passing the practice camps at Pont Rhyd-sarn. Both Jones and Margary identified several lengths of possible *agger*. The OS field investigators agreed with some of these findings.

The road then follows the Wnion Valley. Jones favours the north-west bank and Margary the south-east, while the OS states that 'neither has good evidence although Margary's route is topographically largely impractical'.[104] Jones then traces the route across country via fragments of terrace and a zigzag river crossing to the modern lane leading to Brithdir.

The first part of the route, to the south-west of Caer Gai, was examined during the 2005-6 phase of the Roman Roads Project. The line of the road was initially identified by geophysical survey running through fields to the south-west of the fort on a different alignment to the former driveway to Caer Gai farm.[105] **PRN 17650**. The road then appears to fork with the northern branch, visible on an aerial photograph and Environment Agency lidar, heading towards Tomen y Mur (RR68), and the southern branch extending along modern roads as far as Pont Rhyd-sarn.[106]

There is only one deviation from the modern road, and that is between Pont Lliw and Prys-mawr **SH86913031**. It is now a well-made farm track with no surviving signs of Roman engineering. A slight hollow to the north of the farmhouse marks the line of the earlier road and a slight bank appears to continue across the field to the south-west.

[continued on page 69]

103 Jones GDB, 1959. 'Roman Merionethshire: The Roman Road West of Caer Gai', *BBCS* XVIII Pt.II pp.208-220 / Margary ID, 1955/57. *Roman Roads in Britain*, revised ed. 1967 pp.347-8

104 OS linear files RR66b 1973

105 Hopewell D and Burman J, 2007. 'Geophysical Survey at Caer Gai and Cefn Caer, Pennal Roman Forts', *Archaeology in Wales* 47 pp.91-3

106 Information from Hugh Toller

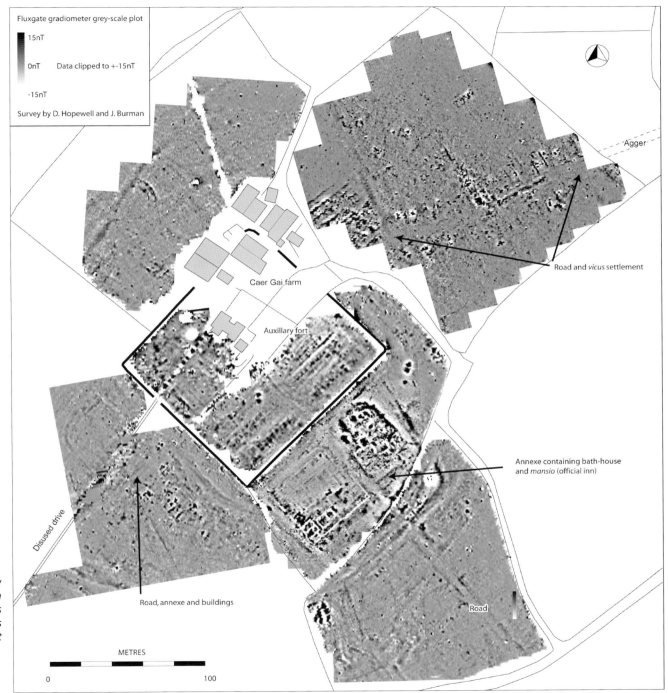

Fluxgate gradiometer grey-scale plot

15nT

0nT   Data clipped to +-15nT

-15nT

Survey by D. Hopewell and J. Burman

Agger

Road and *vicus* settlement

Caer Gai farm

Auxillary fort

Annexe containing bath-house
and *mansio* (official inn)

Disused drive

Road, annexe and buildings

Road

*Geophysical survey
of Caer Gai Roman
fort showing roads
and buildings
outside the fort*

METRES

0   100

The flat, slightly sunken remains of the turnpike road near Pont Rhyd-sarn, PRN 17645

The earlier road deviates from the modern just to the south-west of Pont Rhyd-sarn. It is initially visible as a 5m wide flat-topped causeway **PRN 17645** with stone edging and one roadside ditch, before becoming a sunken road between banks. Despite being a well-preserved 5m wide road this is a typical turnpike road. Although this superficially resembles a Roman road, the causeway is very flat-topped and the sunken road is atypical and not the result of erosion. These are the remains of the eighteenth century turnpike and are a good illustration of the features that can be found on a well preserved example. The road then continues **PRN 17644** as an asphalt track as far as Tan-y-ffordd, before reverting to a flat sunken lane through unimproved pasture and forestry.

As the road emerges from the rough ground into improved pasture to the south-east of Bryn Glas, its character changes and a 5m wide *agger* with slight side ditches can be seen. This could be interpreted in one of two ways. It could be the surviving remnants of a Roman road with the later turnpike removed or ploughed away. Alternatively, it could be the remains of a turnpike, which when ploughed down closely resembles a Roman road. Slab-roofed culverts that seem to be a feature of turnpike roads were also recorded along this stretch. A good example of an *agger* **PRN 17643** close to Pant Gwyn, that was recorded by both Margary and Jones, has since been destroyed by road improvements. The somewhat flimsy evidence for a Roman road is supported by the presence of two Roman practice camps to the south of the road. This suggests that the turnpike was built over the Roman

road. Judging by evidence from several other roads, this was a fairly common occurrence. The turnpike and probably the Roman road continue on the line of the modern road as far as Drws y Nant. **PRN 17640 to 17642**. Two short lengths of surviving earlier road **PRNs 17641 and 17639** recorded as probably Roman road by the OS appear to be typical turnpike.[107]

Jones then traces the Roman road along the course of the modern track from Drws y Nant to Lletty Wyn **SH81282178**. There is little sign of an earlier road apart from a track at a stream-crossing near Lletty Wyn. The latter portion of the route (from Lletty Wyn to the fortlet) was traced during the 2004 phase of the Roman Roads Project. The line of the possible Roman road runs along a range of post-medieval tracks and roads. The general line and width of the tracks suggest a Roman origin but few if any features are visible to prove this. A zigzag **SH79872012** running to the crossing point of the Afon Celynog predates the currently used road and packhorse bridge and could be Roman. There are also signs of a possible ford on the south-west side of the river at this point. The road continues along the line of the modern lane to the fortlet at Brithdir. RRN51 branches off 1.8km to the east of the fortlet.

The line of this road is fairly convincing because it follows the only topographically practicable route. The structural evidence is somewhat meagre but is supported by the presence of practice camps at Pont Rhyd-sarn and 'link road' RRN51.

---

107 OS Linear Files RR66b 1978

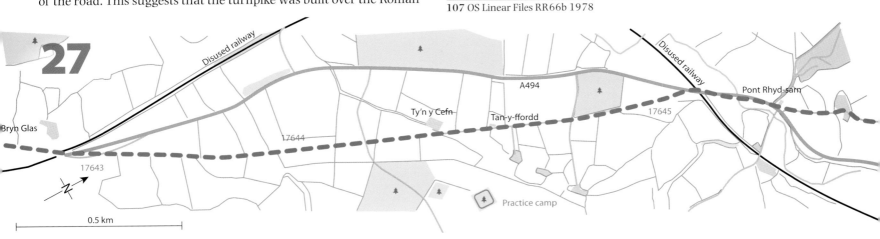

Map 3
page 25

Road RR66a
Caer Gai — Deva (PRN 3850)

Only a portion of this road falls within Gwynedd. The route has been proposed and traced in various places by Margary, Jones and Irvine.[108]

The road immediately to the east of the fort is visible as a low *agger* or as changes in vegetation across the fields as far as the houses at Lôn. It then follows a terrace around the hillside and crosses the Afon Llafar via an *agger* that is visible on Environment Agency lidar survey. It is then thought to run along the narrow corridor of lowland alongside the north side of Bala lake to Llanfor, where all traces have been destroyed by the modern road.

Beyond Llanfor, the OS linear files mark a length of approximately 4km, visible as a well-preserved terrace leading towards Caer Euni, as 'extant'. Also of note are *sarn* place-names, Sarnau and Cefn-ddwysarn. These conclusions were revised when this length of road was examined during the 2005-6 phase of the Roman Roads Project. The road to the east of Llanfor runs along the modern road and trackways until Llidiart-y-groes. At this point the road is carried across an area of boggy ground to Cefn-ddwysarn by a massive flat-topped causeway, 10m wide at the base and 7m wide at the top **SH96433817**. This overlies an earlier road visible as a 5m wide terrace with a hollow way eroded into it **SH96513842**. The causeway appears to be a very impressive example of engineering associated with the turnpike road. The earlier terrace could be an eroded Roman feature or possibly an earlier phase of the turnpike and is probably the origin of Cefn-ddwysarn which translated into English means 'the ridge of the two causeways'. An early phase with Roman characteristics was observed by Edmund Waddelove[109] during pipe-laying works at **SH96153805**.

The road can then be traced for a further 3.2km to Blaen Cwm farm **SH99094015** via Sarnau as a series of low causeways, terraces and slightly sunken lanes. All are about 5m wide and in good condition. There is however little that appears to be Roman. The terraces are massive and stone-revetted, the sunken lanes are sharply-cut and flat-bottomed and the causeways are flat-topped. This is all typical turnpike engineering. According to Margary and Irvine the road from Blaen Cwm to the county border is marked by further terracing, although Irvine suggests a different route to the north of Caer Euni.

This route makes good topographical sense even though much of it is marked by turnpike and modern roads. This is probably another example of a turnpike following a Roman road even though there are few extant Roman features to prove this hypothesis. Definite extant road has, however, been identified, on this alignment, a short distance into Clwyd at Four Crosses and Druid.[110] The general route is therefore correct.

108 Margary ID, 1955/57. *Roman Roads in Britain* revised ed. 1967 pp.77-8 / Jones GDB, 1959. 'Roman Merionethshire: The Roman Road West of Caer Gai', *BBCS* XVIII Pt.II p.215 / Irvine HC, unpublished typescript in OS linear file RR66a dated 1954

109 Burnham BC, Hunter F, Fitzpatrick AP, Worrel S, Hassall MWC & Tomlin RSO, 2005. 'Roman Britain in 2004' *Britannia* Vol.36, pp.387-7

110 Information from Hugh Toller and Toby Driver (RCAHMW AP-2006-3982-5)

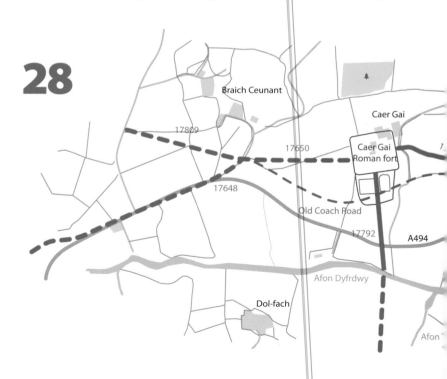

28

The massive sarn at Cefn-ddwysarn is a superb example of turnpike engineering

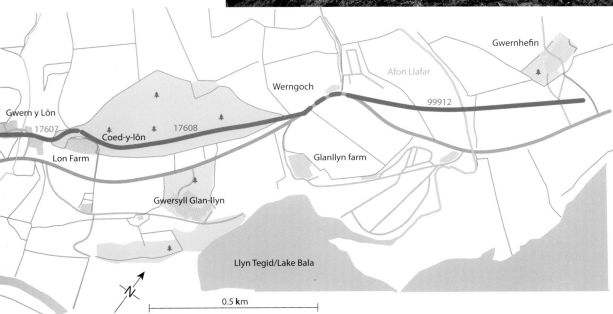

Map 3
page 25

Road RR642
Caer Gai — Caersws

This road was first described by Jones, Putnam and Toller in 1998, with further details published in *A Difficult Road in Deepest Wales* by Putnam & Toller in 2001.[111] This is a particularly good example of the value of detailed fieldwork and sheer persistence in tracing the line of a previously unrecorded road. A more detailed line for the southern-most part was provided by R Knisely-Marpole in a letter to B Silvester of Clwyd Powys Archaeological Trust.

Most of the route within Gwynedd was examined during the Roman Roads Project. The line of the road from the fort running through the annexe and field to the south of the fort has been detected by geophysical survey[112] (*page 67*) and is regularly visible as a parch mark. It then runs across the Dyfrdwy Valley and was identified as a parch-mark on aerial photographs by Toby Driver of the RCAHMW near Dol-Fawr.[113] **PRN 17845**. Fragmentary remains and a straight alignment of hedgerows indicate its line up the south-eastern side of the valley from Felindre to Y Gyrn. The road at the top of the hill then runs through improved but minimally ploughed pasture in the form of a superbly preserved, 5m wide *agger* with side ditches and over 40 quarry pits. It can then be traced as a terrace, running down-slope towards the Fechan valley near Boncyn Crwn cairn.

The cairn, which contains a lot of white quartz stones, appears to have been used by the Romans as a source of stone; the Roman road is edged with similar quartz blocks. The road then runs along a modern track along the eastern side of the Afon Fechan **PRN 17798** before crossing the river and running in to Coed Ty'n-y-fedw forestry plantation where it appears to have been destroyed. The road emerges from the forestry plantation and continues as a well-preserved 4m wide terrace before linking to the modern track to Bwlch y Pawl. A possible milestone was recorded by Putnam & Toller.[4] This is an anomalous large undressed natural stone lying close to the road and could do with further investigation. The road is then visible as fragments of terrace through Bwlch y Pawl, well preserved in places, amongst parallel hollow ways along a clearly multiperiod route towards the Eiddew valley. The line is lost in blanket bogs just before the county boundary.

111 Jones GDB, Putnam WG & Toller HS, 'Roman Road, Caersws to Caer Gai', *Archaeology in Wales* 38, pp.117-19 / Putnam WG & Toller H, 2001. *Archaeology of the Roman Empire, A tribute to the life and works of Professor Barri Jones*, ed. N J Higham, BAR Int. Series 940 pp.117-21

112 Hopewell D & Burman J, 2007. 'Geophysical Survey at Caer Gai and Cefn Caer, Pennal Roman Forts', *Archaeology in Wales* 47 pp.91-3

113 AP-2006-2785 and 4043

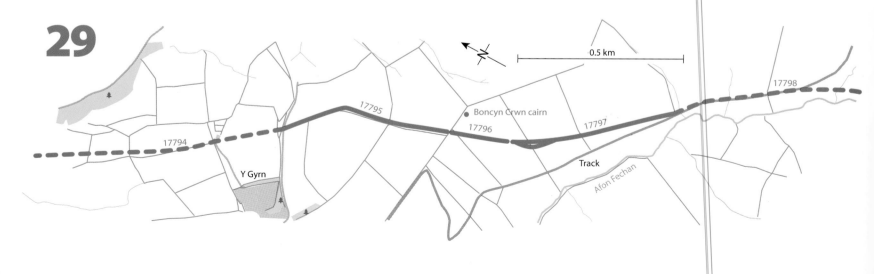

29

0.5 km

17795
Boncyn Crwn cairn
17796
17797
17798

17794

Y Gyrn

Track
Afon Fechan

The well preserved agger at Y Gyrn, heading towards Caer Gai fort on the north side of the valley. PRN 17795

(PHOTOGRAPH: JOHN BURMAN)

Road RRX61
Llanfor — Forden Gaer

Map 3
page 25

This route was initially traced by Harry Longueville Jones[114] with further work by RCAHMW.[115] Some additional evidence was provided by the discovery of the fort at Llanfor, although it seems likely that the fort dates from the initial invasion of north Wales and therefore precedes the construction of the road system.[116]

Both Jones and RCAHMW trace an ancient trackway called Sarn from about 2km east of Llanfor to Trum y Sarn and beyond. It is visible as a series of hollow ways and terraces tracing a line roughly south-east from Llanfor across the uplands of Moel Cae-Howel and Foel Cwm-Sian Llŵyd. The OS field investigation recorded various earthworks and concluded that the route is ...

> ... *probable, and though it has no specifically Roman features* [it] *is comparable to several recognised stretches of Roman road in Wales.*[117]

The parts of this road that run through unimproved pasture were examined as part of the 2004 phase of the Roman Roads project. The road to the north of Bwlch y Fenni **SH97213328** is well-defined and clearly of some antiquity. It consists of a series of hollow ways and terraces, all about 3m wide. These are occasionally rock-cut and the bedrock is worn and rutted where exposed. The road follows the contours around the hill at Rhiweaedog-is-arfon and can be traced for several kilometres through the uplands to Carnedd Wen on the county border **SH99833090**. It is again in the form of a 3m wide terrace, with hollow ways in the more level ground. This road seems to be too narrow to be classified as a Roman military construction without other supporting evidence; no surviving *agger*, roadside ditches or quarry pits are present. This appears to be a road that has been well used in antiquity but there is nothing to suggest Roman origins and it is best interpreted as being medieval or post-medieval. This road was considered to be of sufficient importance to be marked on Evans's 1797 Map of Wales.

Road RRX73
Brithdir — Lydham

Map 4
page 26

Several attempts have been made to trace a road south-east from Brithdir. A route was suggested by Putnam following modern roads.[118] The OS described the suggestion as reasonable but the evidence very tenuous.[119] A similar route (in Gwynedd) was proposed by Rigg & Toller but later retracted.[120] The best supporting evidence is the linking road RRN51 (above) suggesting a route over Bwlch Oerddrws.

This is a fairly contentious route but one that cannot be entirely dismissed. Proof of Roman construction to the east of the junction with RRN51 is required in order to differentiate it from turnpike and later roads.

114 Jones HL, 1856.' List of Early British Remains in Wales, No.VII' *Archaeologia Cambrensis* Third Series Vol.2

115 RCAHMW, 1921. *An Inventory of Ancient Monuments in Wales and Monmouthshire* Vol.I *County of Merioneth* p.118

116 Hopewell D & Hodgson N, 2012. 'Further Work at Llanfor Roman Military Complex', *Britannia* Vol.43, pp.29-44

117 CF Wardale, OS linear files RRX61, 1973

118 Putnam WG, 1963. 'Excavations at Y Gaer, Llanfair Caereinion', *Montgomeryshire Collections* LVII, p.22

119 OS linear files RRX73 1977

120 Rigg J & Toller H, 1983. 'A Roman Road from the Long Mountain to Dolgellau and Some Branches', *Britannia* 14 pp.155-65 / Toller H, 1997. 'The Supposed Road from the Long Mountain to Dolgellau', *Britannia* 30 p.299

121 Hopewell D, 1997. 'Archaeological Survey and Excavations at Brithdir', *JMHRS* XII pp.310-33

122 Margary ID, 1967. *Roman Roads in Britain* pp.355-6

123 Jones GDB, 1959. 'Roman Merionethshire: The Roman Road West of Caer Gai', *BBCS* XVIII Pt.II pp.211-2 / St Joseph JKS, 1961. 'Air reconnaissance in Roman Britain, 1958-60', *Journal of Roman Studies* 51 pp.129-30 / Bowen EG & Gresham C, 1967. *History of Merioneth* Vol.1, pp.252-3

124 Rigg J, further information in OS linear RR69b 1977

125 Dodd AH, 1925. 'The Roads of North Wales, 1750 to 1850', *Arch Camb* LXXX Pt.1 pp.121-48

Road RR69b part 2
Brithdir — Cefn Caer, Pennal
(east of Cader Idris)

Map 4
page 26

There are several predicted road alignments around the fortlet at Brithdir, few of which have been verified. Some reflect the idea that Dolgellau was seen as the main node in the road system in this area, prior to the discovery of the fortlet. The excavations at Brithdir confirmed that there was an east-west road that continued in use after the abandonment, in AD120, of the industrial remains associated with the fortlet.[121] There are two main suggested routes to Cefn Caer, Pennal (*southern Gwynedd map, page 23*). The first, RR69b, was proposed by Margary and runs to the east of Cader Idris.[122] The second, (RRX96 see below), runs to the west and was favoured by Jones, St Joseph and Bowen & Gresham.[123]

The immediate route south from Brithdir is unclear but may simply follow RRN51 to the east. Margary then traces a fairly direct course from Brithdir along Cefn y Clawdd and then an old road across the highlands to the Llefenni Valley. The OS recorded that the route was very eroded and probably not Roman.[124] A very recent discovery by Hugh Toller on Environment Agency lidar survey shows a 0.5km long, straight feature running in a north to south alignment at **SH76471639**, to the west of the modern A487 road to the south of Cross Foxes. Slight features to the north and south of this could represent further lengths of road and may suggest yet another possible route to Cefn Caer, Pennal via Corris. The feature is a very slight earthwork that is almost impossible to trace amongst the rushes and long grass in this area. Systematic probing along its line showed it to be a 4.5 to 5m wide feature that is less than 20cm below the ground surface. A small test-pit revealed a stone and gravel surface that appears to be sitting on a deep accumulation of peat. This seems to be a similar style of construction to that discovered on road RR69a above Cwm Penamnen. More work is needed, however, before this can be considered to be a proven Roman road and excavations are planned for late 2013. Even without excavation this is one of the more convincing pieces of evidence on the numerous proposed routes to the south of Brithdir and adds weight to the

hypothesis that the route lies to the east of Cader Idris.

The route along Cefn y Clawdd is much changed from when recorded by Margary and the Ordnance Survey. The most recent line of the old track has mostly been superseded by a narrow asphalt road. Occasional lengths of earlier road have survived and have not been affected by the recent upgrade. In most cases it takes the form of a terrace with the modern road overlying part of it, although hollow ways also survive in places. At **SH76071402** the modern track curves away from the earlier line. A 4m wide terrace and a possible *agger*, 5m wide, follow the more direct route. At **SH75911366** a 4m wide terrace is cut by a narrow hollow way. There was clearly a well-constructed road of some antiquity running along this route and it was never turnpiked.[125] The fragmentary remains make it difficult to confirm its Roman origins but this route should not be dismissed. Margary next traces the road along the Llefenni valley through Corris and then along the Dovey Valley to Cefn Caer, Pennal. Nothing has subsequently been identified as being Roman and the OS concluded that there was no Roman road along an alignment to the east of Cader Idris and instead favoured the western route, RRX96.

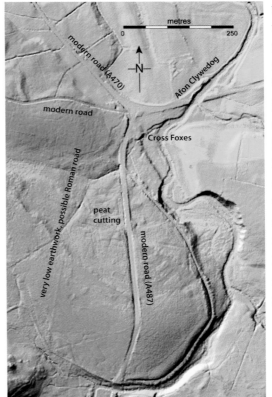

A lidar survey of road RR69b (see page 75)

Environment Agency lidar composite 2012

Road RRX96
Brithdir — Cefn Caer, Pennal
(west of Cader Idris)

Map 4
page 26

Jones, St Joseph and Bowen & Gresham have all published papers dismissing the route of RR69b to the east of Cader Idris, based on unsuitable terrain and the siting strategy of the fortlet at Brithdir.[126] Various possible courses are suggested following a more circuitous route to the west of the mountain. The OS surveyors recorded that none of the routes show any trace of Roman construction. Three variations were proposed; all three initially run south-west from Brithdir along an old turnpike road called the Ffordd Ddu. St Joseph suggested a route extending as far west as the coast at Llwyngwril. Bowen and Gresham traced an inland route along an old road to Llanegryn. A route between Llanegryn and Cefn Caer, Pennal, is favoured by both St Joseph and Bowen and Gresham. Its historical importance is demonstrated by the presence of motte-and-bailey castles at crossings of the Afon Dysynni and Afon Fathew. An alternative shorter route was also proposed by Bowen and Gresham, running across the highlands via Abergynolwyn. The OS note that this road should be visible on the slopes of Mynydd Cefn Caer, but there is nothing more than a narrow footpath at this point.[127]

The initial 2km of road to the west of Brithdir was field-walked during the Roman Roads Project. A 4 to 5m wide road, with many post-medieval features, can be traced following a fairly direct route to the Afon Wnion. The road immediately to the west of the fort is largely lost within improved pasture, although the former owner Mr Edwards of Tyddyn Derwen reports that a parch mark was visible below the modern road in the dry summer of 1976. The road to the west of this is visible as a 4 to 6m wide hollow way bounded for much of its length by field walls **SH76311862**. A well preserved 4m wide zigzag at **SH75791854** of Roman character marks the start of the descent toward Llwybr-y-torrent. Further zigzags mark the crossing of a steep-sided stream on the edge of Coed Dol-fawr. Masonry on the edge of the stream is all that remains of a built-up ford or culvert. This remains

undated but is most likely to be part of post-Roman improvements to the road. This length of road could be Roman, but cannot be proven to be so on current evidence.

All of the proposed routes then follow the Ffordd Ddu running between Dolgellau and Llanegryn. This is a complex multiphase routeway: parts may have a prehistoric origin and it may have been use as a drover's road. There are also lurid tales of smugglers and brigands in the area. It was definitely a turnpike, although apparently not always very well maintained.

Richard Fenton records in 1808 that:

> The Road, which though paid for, and meant for a turnpike, begins to lose all pretensions to such a Character, being rough, stony, and in many parts hardly traceable, and taking its course up very steep pitches; then going on tolerably straight.[128]

He took the old route to Peniarth and recorded that a new road was being built here, probably indicating that there was more than one phase of turnpike:

> The new Road is marked out to turn that projecting point which hides the junction of the Vales, but is not yet in a state to be used.[129]

The northern end of the Ffordd Ddu is now an asphalt-surfaced minor road that runs from Dolgellau up into the highlands by the Cregennan lakes. An earlier terrace, almost certainly a turnpike, deviates from the line of the modern road in several places. The Ffordd Ddu deviates from the modern asphalt road near Hafod Taliadau **SH65661339** and continues as a modern track. The modern track probably incorporates the latest phase of turnpike in many places. This often overlies earlier phases, most notably to the south of Pant-y-llan where the turnpike follows the line of the modern road before diverging to form a zigzag up a steep hillside **SH64901291**. An earlier road, in the form of a hollow way with traces of a possible *agger* in places, approaches this from the north. The turnpike clearly overlies the early road at the bottom of the zigzag. At least two phases of pre-turnpike road also zigzag up the hill with the turnpike. One is quite narrow and overlies an earlier feature that could be a more direct road.

Further to the south-west from **SH64401237**, long stretches of an earlier road run alongside the modern track. The road through Cwm-llwyd is marked as a track on 1888 OS maps but is currently in the form of a very deeply eroded terrace. This substantial feature can be seen to overlie a 4m wide well-engineered terrace in two places, **SH63371009** and **SH62870974**. The modern road and earlier tracks diverge at Foel Tyr Gawen **SH62270780**. The earlier routes run to the west of the hill and two phases are again present. The modern track runs to the east and is probably the new road described by Pennant. The earliest phase of road on this route (i.e. underlying the turnpike) could represent the line of the Roman road. It is at least 4m wide and well-engineered. There is however a distinct possibility that it is instead another phase of turnpike.

The southern leg of this route is more problematic. Much of the line between Rhyd-yr-onen **SH61580217** and Cwrt **SH68790013** was examined in the 2006 season. This was mostly found to be a typical narrow winding pack-horse route with no evidence for Roman engineering. A length of well-engineered wider road was identified on the descent to Cwrt but further evidence is needed before this could be considered Roman.

The various proposers of this route suggested diversions from the Ffordd Ddu. Bowen and Gresham trace a line along a track a little to the west via Allt-lwyd that is flanked by prehistoric remains, suggesting it is early. They also suggest a more direct route to the east, over the uplands via Abergynolwyn. St Joseph suggested a diversion even further to the west via Llwyngwril. No signs of Roman engineering have been discovered on any of these routes.

In conclusion, there are signs of what could be Roman engineering on the route to the west of Cader Idris, but nothing that can be proven. The roads between the other forts in north-west Wales are around 17-20km long, representing a day's march. A direct route between Brithdir and Cefn Caer, Pennal, would be 22km. The route being examined here is a rather excessive 32km long suggesting that units travelling between the forts would have to spend a night in the open. This would seem to negate the advantages of following the slightly easier terrain.

The longer route would make more sense if there was a Roman presence west of Cader Idris. The only hint that this could be the case is in a document in the Peniarth Manuscripts written around 1560 in the hand of the poet Gruffudd Hiraethog. This records a building 'where the bricks are yet to be seen' with paving after the fashion of flint dice and windows in the earth. The flint dice could be interpreted as being *tesserae*, suggesting a Roman mosaic.[130] The location of the building would appear to be close to Peniarth, but there are no further records and its exact location has been lost. If this was indeed a Roman building the road would make more sense. Otherwise the route to the west of Cader Idris seems to be a long diversion and the more direct route RR69b would be more credible. Several other direct routes through difficult terrain have been identified elsewhere in Gwynedd and these seem to be favoured over long diversions through easy terrain. Unfortunately neither route has provided any definitive evidence, which is somewhat surprising since both run through unimproved land for much of their routes. The newly discovered lidar evidence for the eastern route may yet prove to be decisive but further research is required.

126 Jones GDB, 1959. 'Roman Merionethshire: The Roman Road West of Caer Gai', *BBCS* XVIII Pt.II pp.211-2 / St Joseph JKS, 1961. 'Air reconnaissance in Roman Britain, 1958-60', *Journal of Roman Studies* 51 pp.129-30 / Bowen EG & Gresham C, 1967. *History of Merioneth* Vol.1, pp.252-3

127 OS linear file RRX96 1977

128 Fenton R, 1917. *Tours in Wales, 1804-1813*, ed. J Fisher. *Archaeologia Cambrensis* supplementary volume p.107

129 ibid p108

130 RCAHMW, 1921. *An Inventory of Ancient Monuments in Wales and Monmouthshire* Vol.I *County of Merioneth* pp.93-94

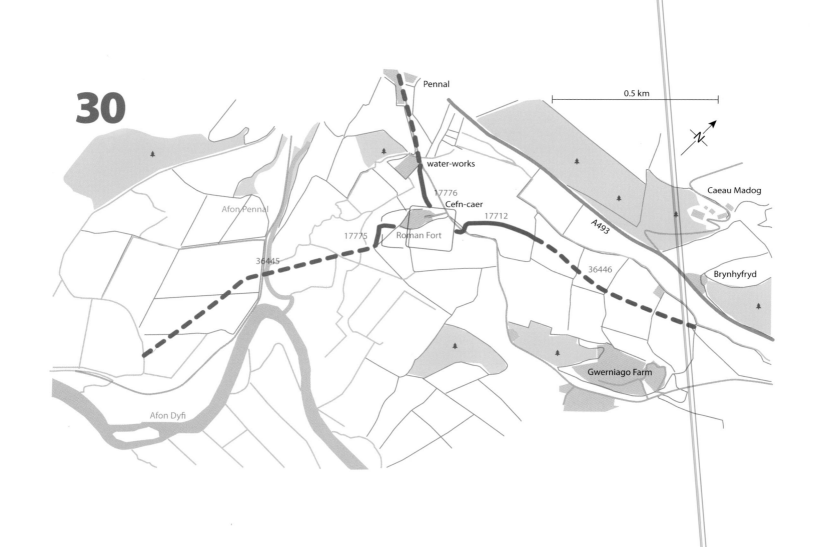

30

Pennal

water-works

17776

Cefn-caer

17712

17775

Roman Fort

Afon Pennal

36445

Afon Dyfi

A493

36446

Caeau Madog

Brynhyfryd

Gwerniago Farm

0.5 km

Map 4
page 26

Road RR69c
Cefn Caer, Pennal — Llanio

The fort at Cefn Caer, Pennal, is in southern-most Gwynedd. A road presumably runs south, crossing the flood-plain of the Dovey, before heading towards the fort at Trawscoed (the river is also the county boundary). There are some rather enigmatic references to a road running directly to the river, the first in 1693 by Maurice Jones, rector of Dolgellau, in a letter to Edward Lhuyd.[131] The remains appear to have been well-preserved at this time:

> *From the Fort to the water-side there is to this day a broad hard way*
> *paved with stones 10 to 12 yards broad in a straight line made through*
> *the marsh ground and meadow lands to the River side which is in*
> *length about 200 yards.*

Richard Fenton visited the site in 1804[132] and recorded that the Vicar of Towyn had seen the causeway running from Cefn Caer to the 'ford-able part of the Dyfi opposite Garreg'. Fenton revisited the site four years later and 'could see no antient pitched way, unless the modern road to the River pursues the same Line'.[133]

Gradiometer survey shows that the road from the fort leads in the direction of the present farm track towards the river. Probing showed that it still retains a solid stony surface beneath modern deposits where the track runs onto the flood-plain. It currently only continues for a short distance but the 1888 25" OS map shows it running as far as the Afon Pennal just before it joins the Dovey. The Environment Agency lidar survey shows a continuation of the feature beyond the Afon Pennal as far as the channel of the Dovey.[134] **Map 30, PRN 36445.** This is also faintly visible on *Bluesky* 2006 and *Getmapping* 2009 aerial coverage and was reported by Professor Barri Jones as a parchmark in the dry year of 1976.[135] It can be seen on the ground as a change of vegetation, with grass instead of rushes growing on the possible road. This may well be the 'broad hard way' and it can be traced for over 800m, considerably further than the 200 yards that were visible in 1693.

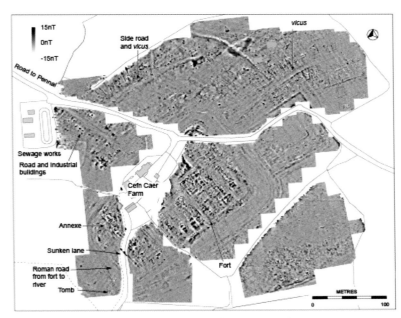

Geophysical survey of the Roman fort at Cefn Caer, Pennal

131 Bodleian Library, Ms *Ashmole*, 1815, fo.265

132 Fenton R. 1917. *Tours in Wales, 1804-1813*, ed. J Fisher. *Archaeologia Cambrensis supplementary volume* pp.52-53

133 ibid p.85

134 Information from John Burman

135 Goodburn R. 1976. 'Roman Britain in 1975; 1. Sites explored', *Britannia* 7 p.296

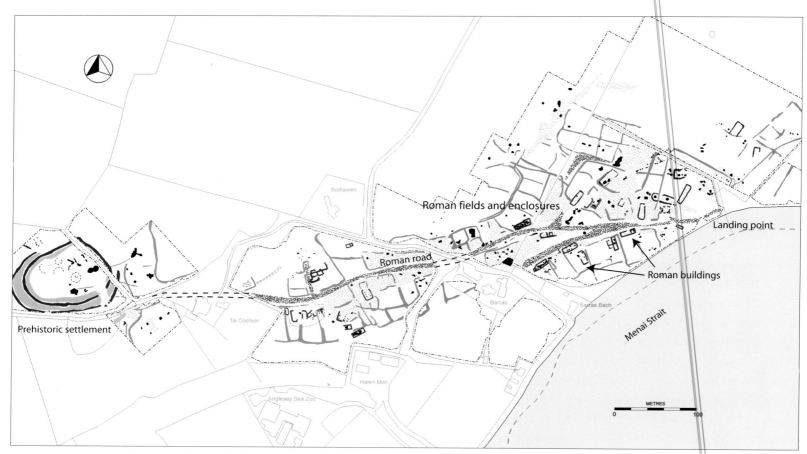

A plan of the Roman trading settlement near Brynsiencyn on the shore of the Menai Strait, from geophysical survey

Roman Roads on Anglesey

Until recently there were no widely accepted Roman remains on Anglesey apart from the watchtowers and late 'naval base' near Holyhead. These two sites are of limited use in the present study because they post-date the establishment of the road and fort network in north Wales. The ditch and bank of a possible fort at Aberffraw on the west coast were identified by White, but the small scale of the excavations and lack of datable evidence leave the interpretation of these features open to debate.[136] The site is also largely built over, which makes the acquisition of further evidence difficult.

Roman roads elsewhere in Wales run between fixed points defined by forts. Unfortunately on Anglesey these basic starting points are unknown. The task of finding Roman roads is further complicated by the topography and agricultural regime on the island. There are no tracts of untouched desolate uplands and almost all of the land is heavily improved.

Geophysical Survey and excavation in 2009-11 by Gwynedd Archaeological Trust revealed the crossing point of the Menai Strait from Segontium.[137] This consists of a wide Roman road, and an extensive civilian settlement. The gravel road surface was the first thing to show up during the excavation running inland from the shore. It is not known for sure if this marks the beginning of a road across Anglesey because the evidence can only be traced with certainty for 0.75km and projected to a possible 2.6km. Its currently projected line would have lead to a difficult crossing of the Malltraeth marshes.

It is likely that further Roman infrastructure existed on Anglesey in the form of roads and at least one fort. Anglesey was of great symbolic value, as the last refuge of the Britons fleeing from the Roman invasion. It was also of economic value as a grain producer and probably for its deposits of copper. It therefore seems likely that the Romans would have garrisoned the island. Tacitus records that Paulinus at least started this process during the invasions of AD60. Temporary camps associated with the well-documented crossing of the Menai Strait during both invasions would also seem to be likely. Further work is clearly needed.

The surface of the Roman road (foreground) was the first feature to show up during the excavations near Brynsiencyn

136 White RB, 1979. 'Excavations at Aberffraw, Anglesey, 1973 and 1974', *BBCS* XVIII pp.319-42

137 Hopewell D, 2011. 'Tai Cochion and Trefarthen Roman Settlement', *Archaeology in Wales* 50 pp.93-4, and forthcoming, *Archaeologia Cambrensis*

Other proposed routes

Most of the routes described by Edmund Waddelove in *The Roman Roads of North Wales, Recent Discoveries* are alternatives to already published routes described elsewhere in this book.[138] He also proposed three major additional roads. The first, a road running along the Ogwen Valley, raises some interesting possibilities.[139] This could have provided access to the uplands of Snowdonia and been linked to slate production. Roman roofing slates from north Wales have been identified as far afield as the fort at Chester, demonstrating some activity within the valleys of northern Snowdonia. The slate was from the Cambrian Period formation that extends from Llanllyfni to Bethesda via Cwm Gwyrfai and Llanberis. Gwynfor Pierce Jones considers it most likely that they came from the Nantlle valley, but modern workings have destroyed almost all traces of early quarrying, so other locations should not be discounted.[140]

There are two other major new alignments proposed in this work. The first runs from Segontium to Nefyn and appears, in part, to follow the pilgrim's route to Bardsey.[141] The road follows the narrow pass between the peaks of Yr Eifl and shows no evidence of Roman engineering. The second road runs between Porthmadog and Dolgellau via Harlech.[142] There are some interesting possibilities on this route, but again most of the roads and trackways described do not have any Roman characteristics.

The revival of the idea of a fort at Dolgellau based on the grid-like pattern of the town's streets makes little sense. The faint pattern of the internal roads of a Roman fort would not have persisted, for well in excess of a thousand years, to influence the establishment of the current street pattern.

---

138 1999, self-published

139 ibid pp.77-101

140 Pierce Jones G & Shakespeare M, 2011. 'Roman Slate Hoard – Llidiart Yspytty, Tremadog Gwynedd. A technical appraisal', in Parry LW et al, 2013, *A487 Porthmadog, Minffordd and Tremadog Bypass. Report on archaeological mitigation*, GAT Report 1065, unpublished, p.8 / See also summary by Pierce Jones G, in Parry LW & Kenney J, forthcoming, 'Archaeological Discoveries along the Porthmadog Bypass', *Archaeology in Wales*

141 Waddelove, 1999. pp.247-277

142 ibid pp.295-327

CONCLUSIONS AND RESEARCH PRIORITIES

The Roman Roads Project has drawn together all of the reliable evidence for Roman roads in Gwynedd. New information is, however, continually emerging, so it is best seen as a snapshot of our understanding at the time of publication. The outline maps provide a good overview of the strengths, weaknesses and reliability of the currently available information.

Things have clearly progressed since the first Ordnance Survey map of the Roman roads of Britain in 1924 and much new information has been added to Margary's overview.

In the north much of the main road between Segontium and Canovium can now be reliably traced, although there are still significant gaps between Pentir and the turn to the uplands at Gorddinog and on the descent to the Conwy valley. There is still a possibility of an undiscovered fort or fortlet on this long and strategically important route. The tracing of the line along the eastern end of the coastal plain, the only possible remaining area where an additional station could be sited, must therefore be seen as a major research priority.

Lidar imagery has produced the first credible evidence for a road running south from Segontium and the general line of the road as far as Pen Llystyn is now reasonably well-established. The continuation of the road south-east to Tomen y Mur is considerably less certain. Roman remains at Tremadog may indicate the general route but no extant road has so far been discovered, apart from the immediate approaches to Tomen y Mur. A more direct line from Segontium to Tomen y Mur, Margary's road RR68, has not been supported by evidence on the ground and now seems to be little more than a product of the understanding of roads prior to the discovery of Pen Llystyn. This does, however, leave the majority of

northern Snowdonia without a Roman presence. This may be a result of a strategy that considered a ring of forts around the uplands to be sufficient. This is not, however, proven and potential routes through the major valleys, in particular the Ogwen as suggested by Waddelove, require further research.

The route of the road south from Canovium via Bryn y Gefeiliau as far as Dolwyddelan is mostly a series of hypothetical projections based on topographical features. The northern part, presumably along the Conwy valley, may well have been destroyed by modern roads, but there is some potential for the discovery of surviving road from parch-marks or chance finds. It is presumed that much of the road to the south, and perhaps to the north, of Bryn y Gefeiliau runs through uncultivated uplands and there is potential for further research there.

Tomen y Mur is the focus for several roads in central Gwynedd. Much of the land in this area has not been affected by intensive agriculture. Roman roads therefore survive very well and recent evidence from aerial photographs, field-work and lidar imagery has filled in some of the gaps left by earlier researchers. The road to the north can be traced as far as Cwm Penamnen near Dolwyddelan, even though the most remote parts are buried beneath deep peat. Almost all of the road running west to Caer Gai can now be traced on the ground as a series of terraces and lengths of low *agger*.

The northern part of the road to Brithdir is mostly well-documented but despite extensive work by several different researchers, the route south of Pen-y-stryd remains unproven. There is no obvious direct topographical route to Brithdir from this point and, as noted above, several potential routes have been proposed. Some were influenced by the possibility of a fort at Dolgellau, before the discovery of the fortlet at Brithdir, which lies further to the east. The proposed eastern routes pass through unimproved uplands so the potential for locating surviving road must be high. The western route, the line of a former turnpike, runs through the extensive forestry plantations of Coed y Brenin; the disturbance caused by both the road and the forestry plantation reduce the chances of discovering undisturbed archaeology. Continued research along the proposed routes should eventually discover some diagnostic evidence.

The other focus for roads in central Gwynedd is Caer Gai. The general line of the road heading north-east towards Deva (Chester) is fairly well documented. The road close to the fort can be traced as an earthwork or as a feature on lidar survey. The remainder in Gwynedd runs either through improved pasture or appears to have been used as the foundation for a turnpike road. There is still however some potential for the discovery of surviving road in farmland. Its general line is proved by extant road at Druid just to the north-east of the border with Gwynedd. A suggested road, branching to the south-east from Llanfor appears to be post-Roman. The line of the road heading south-east from Caer Gai towards Caersws has been well researched and is, in places, very well preserved. It can be traced as far as Vyrnwy, over the border in Powys.

The roads in northern and central Gwynedd are fairly well understood. The same cannot be said for the south of the county. The focus to the south of Tomen y Mur and Caer Gai is the fortlet and associated remains at Brithdir. The presence of a fortlet as opposed to a full-sized fort has never been adequately explained and the lines of the roads running in all directions from the site are somewhat conjectural. The only length of proven road (RRN51) in the area bypasses the fort entirely. Recent discoveries of a well-defended camp and a possible length of road near Cross Foxes to the south suggest that the Roman road may have followed a fairly direct route south to Cefn Caer, Pennal, down one of the valleys to the east of Cader Idris. This does not, however, appear to tie in to the bypass to the east. The bypass could indicate that there is a road running to the south-east (RRX73) but all remains on this route appear to be turnpike. The proposed roads to the west of Cader Idris seem to be increasingly unlikely, unless there is an undiscovered Roman military installation on the route. It no longer seems that the Roman military road builders would have been deterred by the difficulty of the terrain on the eastern route. The upland routes around Tomen y Mur, demonstrate that the steep and boggy uplands of north-west Wales were no obstacle in the search for a direct route between forts.

Further research around Brithdir is clearly essential to our understanding of the Roman roads in the south of the county. Only a single short length of road in the southern part of Gwynedd has so far been proven to be Roman. All the rest are either projections based on topographic factors or are features that are assumed, but not proven, to have Roman origins. The Roman industrial buildings at Brithdir have been partly excavated but the overall layout of the site is poorly understood and the fortlet itself remains undated. Research priorities in the area include the positive identification of extant Roman roads running to Brithdir and a systematic investigation of the area around the fortlet.

At the far south of the county, lidar imagery shows signs of roads running to the east and south of the fort at Cefn Caer, Pennal, in the far south of Gwynedd, but there are no confirmed roads away from the immediate environs of the fort. There are, as noted above, several possible routes north to Brithdir, of which most run through some tracts of unimproved land. There is clearly scope for further research.

In conclusion, our understanding of Roman roads in Gwynedd has developed considerably since the first overviews by the Ordnance Survey and Margary. Most of the northern part of the area is reasonably well understood, but the south needs more work. Modern techniques such as lidar have opened new avenues of research and the continued work of the RCAHMW aerial reconnaissance team has proved to be of great value. The best results have been produced by adopting clear diagnostic criteria and applying them to concentrated research on possible routes, using all available techniques. There is still scope for much further research and there will almost certainly be discoveries that will modify the proposed layout of Roman roads presented in this book ∎